JOBS - APPRENTICE 101

An American Solution

*Creating Jobs, Entrepreneurs
& Reducing Poverty*

Arthur W. Hoffmann, Ed.D.; P.E.

iUniverse, Inc.
Bloomington

JOBS - APPRENTICE 101
AN AMERICAN SOLUTION

Copyright © 2012 by Arthur W. Hoffmann, Ed.D.; P.E.

All rights reserved. No part of this book may be used or reproduced by any means, graphic, electronic, or mechanical, including photocopying, recording, taping or by any information storage retrieval system without the written permission of the publisher except in the case of brief quotations embodied in critical articles and reviews.

iUniverse books may be ordered through booksellers or by contacting:

iUniverse
1663 Liberty Drive
Bloomington, IN 47403
www.iuniverse.com
1-800-Authors (1-800-288-4677)

Because of the dynamic nature of the Internet, any web addresses or links contained in this book may have changed since publication and may no longer be valid. The views expressed in this work are solely those of the author and do not necessarily reflect the views of the publisher, and the publisher hereby disclaims any responsibility for them.

Any people depicted in stock imagery provided by Thinkstock are models, and such images are being used for illustrative purposes only.
Certain stock imagery © Thinkstock.

ISBN: 978-1-4759-3132-7 (sc)
ISBN: 978-1-4759-3133-4 (ebk)

Printed in the United States of America

iUniverse rev. date: 06/11/2012

Contents

Dedication		vii
Acknowledgments		ix
Prologue		xiii
Chapter 1	Introduction	1
Chapter 2	Background	3
Chapter 3	Apprenticeship Approach	7
Chapter 4	Apprenticeships—American Way	13
Chapter 5	Apprentice 101—Creating Good Jobs	16
Chapter 6	Jobs Tax Incentive—Investment Example	19
Chapter 7	The Benefits for Skilled People	24
Chapter 8	Entrepreneurs—Business Successes	26
Chapter 9	Trade and Vocational School Expansion	30
Chapter 10	American Education Status	32
Chapter 11	College or General Education Pursuit	38
Chapter 12	America's Cities and Rural Communities	42
Chapter 13	A Poverty Solution—Utilizing Apprentice 101	49
Chapter 14	Endnote	52
Epilogue		55
Appendix		57
Suggested Resources for Further Information		73
References		75
About the Author		77

Dedication

In remembrance of my Mom and Dad, who raised a wonderful supportive family.

My Dad especially, was my Mentor, encouraging honesty, hard work, discipline, and loyalty to family and friends.

This dedication would not be complete without recognizing Carolyn, my wife, companion, and friend. Thank you for your support.

Acknowledgments

I am very grateful for the comments, assistance and proof-reading of the content of this book. Martin ("Marty") Pavlock is a talented friend that I relied upon for his expertise and knowledge about the current state of affairs of our country. Marty spent a great deal of time and effort advising me of potential politically sensitive subjects and I am thankful for his thoughtfulness. In particular, Marty does accounting and tax preparation. The fictitious tax returns for Joe and Tom in the Appendix were his creations.

I also want to acknowledge that much of my research and references were the result of several currently published books and news releases relative to the political environment and especially the subjects of unemployment, underemployment, education, job creation, poverty, and the American dream. In particular the most influential references were:

- "*No Apology*", Mitt Romney, February 2011 Edition;
- "*Back to Work*", Bill Clinton, 2011 Edition;
- "*No They Can't*", John Stossel, 2012 Edition;
- "Newsmax.com,—daily news releases
- "Yahoo!Finance" @ yahoo.com—daily news, and
- "en.wikipedia.org.

A complete list of references is included in the Reference Section.

"Entrepreneurs and their small enterprises are responsible for almost all of the economic growth in the United States"

—*Ronald Reagan*

Prologue

Jobs are the life blood of our economy. They create wealth in exchange for services rendered that increase and improve our way of life. Both the individual and the nation share in the growth and equity that result from this day-to-day activity. The type of work a person does defines his or her social status and enhances their feeling of self-worth. Most Americans strive to become members of what is regarded as "middle-class." To do so requires initiative, basic education, and the development of some personal skill or aptitude. Opportunity is the decisive factor in achieving a person's occupational dream. The American workforce represents every conceivable type of economical pursuit. Every occupation or skill represents a value that is compensated for by fulfilling a human need. Full employment is an indicator of a prosperous and growing national economy, while unemployment is a sign of uncertainty, worry, and despair. Loss of a job can be devastating, not only to the person's self-worth, but to his or her family's security and health.

Today, the many jobless people in America are losing hope of an economic recovery. The American workforce has decreased by several million jobs, yet our population continues to grow. We are told that it is because of a global economy and jobs are fleeing America, and that there is nothing we can do about it! Our politicians, both Republican and Democrat, respond with contrasting solutions that focus only on taxes and spending. Specific solutions to job creation have not been publicized or pursued. I believe that we need to address unemployment and under-employment by direct citizen involvement. The following is a proposed "Jobs Initiative" that will result in immediate job growth and an expansion of the American economy.

CHAPTER 1

Introduction

Recently, severe weather and tornadoes ravaged several states in our Midwest. TV news reports showed the devastation of homes and businesses and heart-wrenching, painful human tragedy. The response to this disaster was a reminder of how Americans typically unite and rally, to assist during a national calamity. We forget politics and personal expense in order to address and solve the crisis. While watching the first responders who assisted during this natural disaster, I was reminded of the value of having trained, skilled workers and volunteers who regularly risk their lives to help the unfortunate in an emergency. These citizen/heroes reside in every community, town, and city in America. As a country, we are blessed to have people who utilize their skills and technology to serve us on a daily basis. Think of the electrical line worker when power is lost; or the firefighter, police officer, medical personnel, or EMS technician. And, let's not forget the skilled trades, electricians, plumbers, carpenters, mechanics, technicians, craftsmen, teachers, road/bridge/infrastructure/contractors—and the list goes on. We could not function without truckers, delivery persons, farmers, food-processors, pharmacists, etc. These typical citizens comprise the working foundation of America. They are the common people who possess the critical skills and unique talents that are the heartbeat of our economy. They are both the producers and consumers of goods and services that generate the equity and value of the nation. Homemakers are the foundation of the American family who in turn motivate the entire economic process. Therefore, everyone is a contributor, regardless of occupation, type of employment, or essential service. This is the foundation of the American workforce. *This is where the real jobs are created.* These workers pay the taxes upon which our economy relies. Predominately, they make-up the so-called "middle-class". Unfortunately, chronic poverty still exists in our country. We need to solve it, and we can accomplish this objective with a sincere commitment by everyone to challenge our current entitlement policies. "Entitlements" are an economic cost, not an investment.

CHAPTER 2

Background

Recently, during the Republican Presidential Primaries, we were exposed to the short-comings of the current Democratic administration. Loss of jobs due to a severe economic downturn is a primary concern of the average American family. The unemployment and under-employment rates were officially hovering at 9%, following massive inoculations of stimulus funds into the economy. The focus of the stimulus money was, for the most part, misdirected and ineffective in creating needed jobs. Actually, rather than creating new (more) jobs, the result was the loss of several millions of jobs, even though the nation's population was increasing. The current Administration, however, re-categorized the jobs stimulus objective to the goal of saving existing jobs. Absent was any specific program or initiative to actually create real jobs to help the American people. What was promised were "shovel-ready" jobs that proved to be non-existent. The President even admitted this fallacy in a remark during an interview (". . . there's no such thing as shovel-ready projects . . . .") (Baker, 2010). The term "shovel ready jobs", has the implication that President Obama believes that manual labor jobs are the road to prosperity. Why not skilled jobs and high technology application opportunities to advance the American workforce?

Actually, the real unemployment statistics were closer to 15% in manufacturing regions of the U.S. Even worse is the job devastation in the inner cities, where poverty is more common. Stimulus funds were not directed to this critical need. Congress instead continued to extend unemployment compensation to 99 weeks without any effort to actually improve the jobs picture. The majority in Congress actually believed that unemployment funds would create prosperity by a mysterious multiplication factor.

The current administration has not offered any *specific* jobs initiative programs that would actually *create* new jobs. The administration's venture into *green* solar-based jobs has been a disaster. A Washingto Post headline stated that, "Obama green jobs cost $5 million each". A Washington Post further reported that "the $38.6 billion loan guarantee program created just 3,545 new permanent jobs" (Grinder, 2011). This equates to $5 million dollars per job. Not only did this misguided effort result in losing jobs, and closing facilities, taxpayers foot the bill for billions of wasted dollars distributed to political donors.

In his new book, *Back to Work* (Clinton, 2011), former President Bill Clinton supports the need for a strong government to ensure a strong economy. The book's title infers that he has a plan(s) for solving our jobless concerns, but no solution(s) are presented. Instead of offering real job opportunities, Clinton reassures readers that the green technology development must move forward. He proposes that the government "reinstate" the expired tax credit for green energy technology jobs that he believes are still a viable alternative to proven energy generation. Clinton also supports the Administration's "shovel ready" infrastructure jobs, but that we need to speed-up the process.

In part two of the book, Clinton offers a list of forty-six (46) ideas of things we can do to get back to the future. Clinton's list includes several "Related—Job Creating Ideas" (Clinton, 2011, 154-183). Some examples are:

- Corporations should bring money back to America;
- Retrofit major buildings (i.e., Empire State Building) to reduce energy use;
- Tax credit for hybrid/electric vehicles;
- Build rapid rail;
- Fill 3 million open jobs that require skilled workers. Employers need to train on-job.
- Stop laying-off workers. Copy German short work-week. Keep skilled workers, and

- Increase role of government Small Business Administration (SBA).

In summary, President Clinton's view for the nation's economic future is dependent on more government involvement and oversight of private business. Clinton's final "back to work" remarks were: "We all need to do what works. And we don't have a day or a dollar to waste" (Clinton, 2011, 187).

Republican Presidential Primary candidates also offered no concrete job-creation ideas. Several candidates only suggested that, through taxes and smaller government, jobs would germinate and grow. There are many factors that influence the economy which ultimately could result in reducing the current high unemployment we are experiencing. (Appendix A). Much of the problem is due to government intrusion into private business. A basic tenet of Conservatism (Republican Party) is that jobs can only be created in the private sector of the economy, especially by small business/entrepreneurs, and not the government. Only Mitt Romney and Herman Cain had the private and public experience to understand the jobs-creation challenge. It is assumed that, if elected, they would enlist the best private industry captains to structure an aggressive program to promote job and economic growth in an expeditious timetable. Hopefully, these experienced business men and women would represent a cross-section of the American economy and focus on proven technology and energy, while providing a fresh influx of leadership that would invigorate Washington D.C. and focus on "real America".

What is needed now is a specific "jobs initiative" effort by private citizens who have the ability and motivation to grow the economy and achieve their dreams. These entrepreneurs would seize an opportunity to expand and grow their business if the Federal, State and local government officials would allow "free-market enterprise" to blossom.

Job growth represents an investment in America. It is time for the "political system" to recognize that the success of the nation is generated by people and can be curtailed by political constraint. Workers and business generate wealth and pay the taxes that provide essential services. Politicians do not create wealth, they diminish it. The focus of government needs to be on investment, not on spending. Investment signifies growth: growth in resources, people, education, training, technology, equipment and proper utilization of our abundant natural resources to increase productivity which, in turn, increases our nation's wealth.

CHAPTER 3

Apprenticeship Approach

The inspiration for this "jobs initiative" is the result of the now famous TV Apprenticeship Series, master-minded by Donald Trump. This celebrated competitive-career challenge drama introduced the public to real-life employee situation resolution. It distinguished the term "Apprentice" and made it a household word representing on-the-job training protocol. Donald Trump used adult business situations to demonstrate the competitive spirit of American prowess to succeed by utilizing a combination of intelligence, mental angst, skill, and practicality to compete against other apprentice candidates and solve the interesting, but fictitious TV job situation challenge.

In real-life, an apprentice is the initial step toward achieving "craftsman" status in any useful discipline. The apprenticeship journey from novice to professional requires development of the same life-long attributes that were displayed in the Trump sagas. Wikipedia describes "Apprenticeship" as "a system of training a new generation of practitioners of a structured competency—based set of skills. Apprenticeships range from craft occupations or trades to those seeking a professional license to practice in a regulated profession". Most of the training is done while working for an employer who helps the candidate learn his or her trade or craft, in exchange for the candidate's continuing labor for an agreed period after the apprentice has achieved measurable competence. Many trades or crafts require a basic education in science, technology, English and math, typically at the high school level. The employer may suggest remedial or technical courses available at local schools that the apprentice can complete concurrently with his/her skill training.

A skilled, competent workforce is essential for national survival and to allow the U.S. to compete in an ever-changing world economy. In order to accomplish this objective, many countries have government-structured apprentice training programs for young people, to ensure that their country has the skilled resources to maintain and advance their economic status. Often the government collaborates with unions and industry organizations to assure a smooth transition from education and training to full-time employment. In Europe, the apprenticeships are integrated within the compulsory 12 year education system, with mandatory career path decisions required in the 9th to 12th year of schooling. Figure # 1 is a schematic of the Romanian Educational System that is currently common in Europe, and especially in the former Eastern Bloc countries.

Apprenticeships—A World View

Many countries around the world utilize structured educational training programs, or apprenticeships that are embedded in their occupational code. Some governments actually pay the salary of regulated apprentices.

Following are examples of apprenticeship requirements of several other countries:

1) Canada

In Canada, each province has its own apprenticeship program. At the completion of the provincial exam they may write the Interprovisional Standard Exam. The interprovisional exam questions are agreed upon by all provinces. The apprentice is then qualified to practice their trade (skill) anywhere in Canada.

2) <u>Germany</u>

Apprenticeships are a part of Germany's dual education system, and as such form an integral part of many people's working lives. Finding employment without having completed an apprenticeship is almost impossible. In Germany there are 342 recognized trades where an apprenticeship can be completed. The dual system means that apprentices spend about 50—70% of their time working, and the rest in formal education. In 2001, two-thirds of young people aged under 22 began an apprenticeship, and 78% of them completed it, meaning that approximately 51% of all young people under 22 have completed an apprenticeship. In 2003, one in three companies offered apprenticeships. In 2004, the government signed a pledge with industrial unions that all companies, except very small ones, must take on apprentices.

3) <u>France</u>

In 2005, President Jacques Chirac announced the introduction of a law on a program for social cohesion comprising the three pillars of employment, housing and equal opportunities. The French government pledged to further develop apprenticeships as a path to success at school and to employment, based on its success: in 2005, 80% of young French people who had completed an apprenticeship entered the workforce. Following the civil unrest at the end of 2005, the government announced a new law. Dubbed "law on equality of chances", it created the "First Employment Contract" as well as apprenticeship for youths as young as 14 years of age. From this age, students are allowed to quit the compulsory school system in order to quickly learn a vocation. This measure has long been a policy of conservative French political parties, and was challenged unsuccessfully by trade unions.

4) Austria

Apprenticeship training in Austria is organized in a dual education system with company-based training of apprentices and complemented by compulsory attendance of a part-time vocational school. The program lasts two to four years and covers 250 legally recognized apprenticeship trades. Qualified students may apply for an Apprenticeship Leave Certificate that provides access to two different vocational careers. By exam they may qualify as a Master Craftsman or Higher Education Entrance that allows them to take up studies at colleges and universities.

5) India

In India, the Apprentices Act regulates programs for the training of young people. The Central Apprenticeship Council allows utilization of facilities available for training in the various industries. The goal is to ensure that the workforce requirements for industry are met.

6) Pakistan

In Pakistan, special apprenticeship programs are established to fulfill the needs of the IT industry. The Pakistan Software Export Board has an attractive program for young IT graduates. The board offers financial subsidy for companies to recruit graduates possessing the basic skills and knowledge in Information Technology. These recruits, who generally start with some experience rather than traditional apprentices, are hired by companies as full-time employees and put through a 12-month in-company training and mentoring discipline. This program resulted in 700 job opportunities.

7) United Kingdom

Apprenticeships have a long tradition in the United Kingdom, dating back to the 12th century and based on Master Guild Craftsman organizations. Apprenticeships are the mainstay of training in U.K. industry, and the reason is to avoid shortages in traditional skilled occupations and higher technician and engineering professionals. In the U.K., apprentice graduates receive either an Ordinary National Diploma (OND) or a Higher National Diploma (HND). Candidates can progress from an OND to a HND with additional educational courses. For entrance to the higher technical engineering apprenticeships, "O" Levels have to include Mathematics, Physics, and English language.

The traditional apprenticeship framework's purpose was to provide a supply of young people seeking to enter work-based learning via programs offering structured high-value learning and transferable skills and knowledge. Apprenticeship training was enabled by linking industry with local technical colleges and professional engineering institutions. As of 2009, there were over 180 occupational apprenticeship programs in the U.K. In England, the government funds 50% of the cost of training apprentices. Employers who offer apprenticeships have an employment contract, including pay-rates with their apprentices. However, off-the-job training and assessment is wholly funded by the state for apprentices aged between 16 and 18.

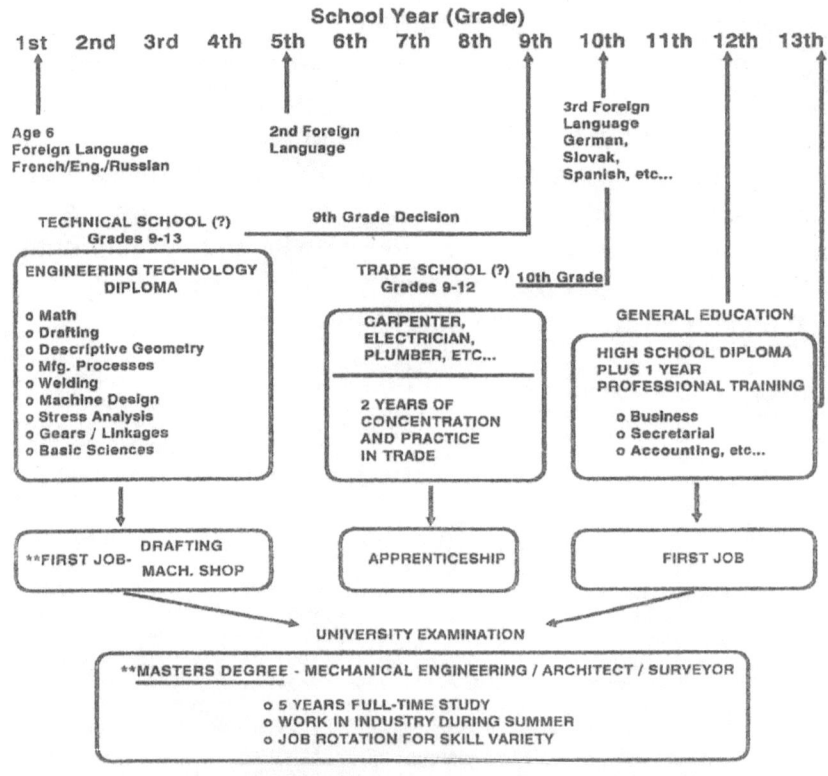

CHAPTER 4

Apprenticeships—American Way

The United States

The United States does not have a structured educational program for trades or crafts, but relies on our free-market system to supply the required workforce skills necessary to maintain our global leadership. As a country, we have been blessed with the freedom and ability to grow our economic strength. This is largely due to private entrepreneurs. It is essential that we rely on the private economy to maintain our National competitiveness for future generations. According to the Internal Revenue Code, the United States has 21 categories of "Job Types" and 317 Job Classifications. For tracking and tax purposes the IRS has assigned six-digit codes for every classified job. The six-digit codes are based on the North American Industry Classification System (NAICS). Figure # 2 shows a condensed summary of the IRS job categories and job codes. (See Appendix A for a complete listing).

Figure No. 2
Sole Proprietorships

IRS Principal Business or Professional Activity Codes
IRS six-digit codes based on the North American Industry Classification System (NAICS).

Code No.	Category	No. of Jobs/Classification
720000	Accommodations / Hotel / Travel / Food Svc	7
560000	Admin. & Support / Waste Mgt / Remediation	18
110000	Agriculture / Forestry / Hunting & Fishing	7
710000	Arts, Entertainment & Recreation	9
230000	Construction of Buildings	25
611000	Educational Services	1
520000	Finance & Insurance	11
620000	Health care & Social Assistance	19
510000	Information	7
310000	Manufacturing, Apparel/Beverage/Tobacco/Textile/Food	16
320000	Manufacturing, Paper/Petro/Coal/Chemical/Nonmetallic	17
330000	Manufacturing, Computer/Electr/Machine/Medical/Transprt.	9
210000	Mining, Coal / Metal Ore / Nonmetal / Oil & Gas Extract.	5
810000	Other Services, Personal/Laundry/Repair & Maintenance	22
540000	Professional / Scientific / Technical Services	23
530000	Real Estate / Rental & Leasing	12
813000	Religious / Civic / Professional & Similar Organizations	1
440000	Retail Trade, Bldg. Matl/Garden/Appliance/Food/Home/Auto	38
450000	Retail Trade, General/Sport/Music/Hobby/Book/Nonstore	22
480000	Transportation & Warehousing	15
490000	Couriers & Messengers / Storage Facilities	2
220000	Utilities	1
420000	Wholesale Trade, Merchant / Durable Goods / Nondurable	27
425000	Wholesale Electronic Markets / Agents & Brokers	2
999999	Unclassified-Unable to classify	1

No. of Job Type Categories = __21__   Total Job Classifications = __317__

Note: The Job Classification System can be very useful in tracking and auditing new job placements and openings as they occur. If we had such a system today we could verify new job placements and have an accurate method of projecting unemployment and current workforce statistics. It would also be possible to use postal mail zones in concert with the job classifications to determine geographic growth areas and type of job placements.

The purpose of an apprentice approach to creating jobs is multi-faceted:

- Typically we envision younger people in a learning role;
- Younger people are bright, and anxious to excel and succeed;
- The recruitment base is large and untapped;
- Young people represent our future;
- Skilled adults are comfortable in their careers and want to share experience;
- Learning is a natural progression;
- It is expedient to transfer skills and craftsmanship from a senior to a junior;
- Expectations of success are very high;
- The cost is minimal and limited to training/education duration; and
- America forever benefits from this investment.

CHAPTER 5

Apprentice 101—Creating Good Jobs

The creation of jobs is the goal of this apprenticeship approach. It is an investment in people-power, and especially in our youth. Well-intentioned citizens have an inherent stake in the growth of the economy and many can directly benefit because they are in a position to so. Every business, large and small, necessarily employs the number of people required to achieve its current goals. However, most businesses desire to expand so as to further ensure their success. This is especially true of the sole owner or independent contractor whose livelihood is totally dependent on his or her earnings potential. Interruption, of the business due to health, accident, or physical ability can be devastating not only for the proprietor, but for his/her family and dependents. However, taking on a helper or another employee may not be financially feasible unless there is a positive incentive to do so. This proposed "apprenticeship approach" is a solution. The "carrot-on-a-stick" would be an investment by the government to help sponsor the hiring of a new wage-earner, as an apprentice, who can advance in the trade or business skill and ultimately become the craftsperson, plumber, electrician, trucker, accountant or any of the 317 "job classifications" currently recognized by the IRS.

The idea is to pay the "learner" a generous salary of $14/hour or more to attract jobless candidates who will strive to be successful in their new venture. Their income will propel them out of the poverty syndrome. It also mandates that the new employee pay federal withholding. The U.S. government allows the entrepreneur a 50% tax credit based on the new employee's salary. The primary investment is made by the entrepreneur who employs the apprentice. This private citizen, or business, takes the "risk", provides the on-job training, mentors the candidate, handles the payroll (including tax and social security deductions) and assures success for the "apprentice" and the business. The U. S. government's minimal "new employee tax credit" investment multiplies substantially over time. This is especially true if the new employee was previously receiving welfare funds, food stamps or other assistance prior to the apprenticeship. The U.S. gains a new generation of taxpaying citizens with marketable skills and practical experience and benefits society forever.

"Apprentice 101" is not intended to require a structured learning sequence similar to mandatory European government programs. Our "apprenticeship" requirements would be determined by the entrepreneur or business enterprise to meet their specific requirements. We are interested in creating useful income-producing jobs. The entrepreneur or employer is responsible for determining the specific job criteria as well as the amount and type of training the apprentice requires based on what is necessary to serve their customers. Jobs are intended to fill an economic need, not to satisfy a politician or bureaucrat's quest for power and influence.

Organized labor, trade unions, and technical training institutions would also form an essential role in the organization of the "jobs initiative" to ensure success. Many trade organizations and unions already have their own structured apprenticeship training programs designed to fit their current and future human resource requirements. The cost of these current programs could also be supplemented by government incentives, and tax benefits provided the net result is a future increase in revenue due to job growth and reduction of poverty. Even greater success would be realized if the private business sector and training institutions would cooperate in delivering common-sense basic educational curriculum for "Apprentice 101" students. An ideal technical school offering: Science, Technology, English and Math ("STEM") would benefit our nation far more than the college education focus that has resulted in a generation of unemployed and underemployed young debtors.

Apprentice Graduates

Graduates of apprentice programs learn much more than an occupational skill. For many this is their first real job. They have to develop discipline that is essential both on and off the job. Responsibility will become a life-long attribute. And most likely for the first time in their lives, their attendance and punctuality will be monitored, with economic consequences for sub-par performance. Also, meaningful relationships will develop among the students and their peers and mentors. Obviously, the job experience becomes the primary attribute.

CHAPTER 6

Jobs Tax Incentive— Investment Example

The "jobs initiative" is designed to expedite job formation by focusing on our skilled workforce to keep our economy expanding and to promote innovation. Businesses, manufacturers, unions, and organizations that sponsor apprentices and have training programs to expand their employee base are ideally suited to take advantage of the "Apprentice 101" initiative. However, any skilled tradesman, craftsman, technician, medical personnel, info-techs, etc., willing to train or mentor an assistant to perform necessary duties and become job-proficient are encouraged to participate in this "jobs solution".

First responders, police, firefighters, nurses and medical personnel are always in critical demand, and training programs and resources are typically available to accelerate new job fulfillment. These are professional and governmental positions that are often restricted by budget or monetary resource concerns, and require the approval of the state or municipal electorate. The proposed jobs solution has specific financial considerations that will promote this unique career position expansion.

The larger workforce expansion is directed toward our special skilled and trained workers. There is a need for an ever-expanding skilled workforce in all conceivable disciplines. This is especially true due to the acceleration of baby-boomer retirement. What is needed is a multi-faceted incentive that will encourage proliferation of immediate job openings. Some of the special attributes of the skilled trades, "boutique" talents, crafts-persons, unique businesses and services are pride, confidence, self-preservation, and a desire to succeed. Individuals employed in these areas strive to excel in whatever job they perform. Some are employees of large or small companies, while many are self-employed or independent contractors. All know they are competent in their job and most are key employees in their company. The owners of these enterprises certainly value their skilled people.

For any business to succeed it must manage its human and financial resources to achieve a secure and profitable balance sheet. To do so, the owner/manager must be vigilant regarding competition, expansion, and attracting as well as retaining critical employees. Therefore, a good manager or entrepreneur will pursue opportunities that will enhance the business. For example, if an employer can hire a new productive employee at a minimum salary and gain productivity or business expansion, he/she certainly will. This "jobs now" program is directed at individuals and businesses that have the ability and desire to expand their workforce by hiring and training people (especially younger persons) to become skilled and productive employees. These apprentices will be very helpful to their employer and community as they gain experience. The cost to the employer would be structured to benefit the employer and the country, while adding a productive employee and taxpayer. The essential incentive is a 50% income tax credit to cover the new employee's salary. The following example illustrates the economics (based on 2011 tax schedule):

Joe, a self-employed carpenter; has a net taxable income for 2011 = $ 100,000.00

Joe & wife Mary file (joint tax return) their **2011 IRS Tax obligation = $ 14,619.00**

Joe decides to hire Tom as an apprentice.

- Joe pays Apprentice Tom a salary of $ 14.00 per hour (50 wks. x 40 hrs.) = $ 28,000.00

Jobs - Apprentice 101

- Joe also pays 1/2 of FICA & Medicare for Tom = $1,582.00
- Joe pays an annual total for Apprentice Tom of = **$29,582.00**
- Joe claims a 50% tax credit for Tom's salary = $14,000.00
- **Joe's final 2011 tax obligation = ($ 14,619 minus $14,000) = $ 619.00**

Joe saved $ 14,000 income tax, because he hired an apprentice.

Carpenter Joe (entrepreneur) hires and trains Apprentice Tom at a cost of $ 7.79 per hour and reduces his tax obligation by $14,000. **However,**

- Apprentice Tom earns = $ 28,000 /yr.
- Tom's income tax obligation (files single) = $ 2,401.00
- Tom also pays FICA and Medicare = **$ 1,582.00**
- Tom pays a total to the government = **$ 3,983.00**

Result: Win—Win:

- **Tom + Joe pay a total of = $ 6,184.00 in Income Tax and FICA**

    Joe w/out Apprentice Tom would have paid the IRS = $14,619.00

    - Therefore hiring Tom cost the U.S. treasury **$8,435.00,** but this is very minimal because:
    - The U.S. gains one (1) new employee with a productive future & with potential Higher future earnings, and paying higher taxes. The U.S. also has an extra contributor to Social Security and Medicare.
    - Carpenter Joe only pays $7.79/hr for an extra OJT (on-job-training) employee.

- Joe, the carpenter, has an extra high potential employee and can increase his business in the future;
- The U.S. does not have to pay Tom unemployment compensation;
- Tom is a new consumer of goods & services.
- **In addition Apprentice Tom pays the State of Michigan income tax = $ 1,057.00**[*]

This is job creation by the people for the U.S. Government, not government down to the people. Typical apprentices learn and practice their skills during a 2 to 4 year period prior to graduation. Following matriculation, the person becomes a high-skilled, productive, tax-paying citizen. (For reference, the Appendix contains sample IRS tax returns for Joe & Tom based on the above analysis). The above example is a basic cost analysis for a *young apprentice who was not receiving any government aid or assistance*. If this young person was receiving government aid and/or food stamp assistance the picture changes dramatically. Research studies show that an unemployed youth (not currently in school or working) could receive an average of $14,000 dollars per year in welfare aid; and $1,596 dollars annually in Supplemental Nutrition Assistance Program (SNAP), formerly food stamps. In this case the U.S. Government would be saving over $7,100 dollars per year for a newly employed apprentice. That would be a great return on investment for the first year alone. Our country would save $7,100 dollars, and get a new taxpayer and FICA contributor to boot.

Skilled people have a bright future with many options. A skilled trade's person or craftsman can work for a large or small company, union or non-union. They can start their own business. They can go back to school or college and become a professional lawyer, doctor or educator. Every option is open. Skilled people are competent, confident, and exhibit self-worth. They comprise the professional and economic pulse of America.

---

* (varies by state)

Invest in Jobs

The objective of the "Apprentice 101" idea is to present the federal and state governments with an alternative approach to new job creation rather than continuing to follow the failed path of unearned entitlement hand-outs. By promoting the apprenticeship route our leaders would be funding an investment, instead of creating a cost burden. There are numerous statistics that confirm employment is the route to prosperity for everyone. Employment in any job category is essential for us to finally attack poverty and the injustice that has been so pervasive since the great depression. Well-meaning politicians have tried to solve these chronic social problems, but they seem to get diverted from the task, in favor of accomplishing their philosophical goals and protecting and retaining their political power base.

Welfare payments in the United States cost $14,700 dollars per person each year, or $70,000 dollars for a family of four. This unearned income is more than the per capita income than most of the rest of the world. Every unemployed youth (someone between 16 and 24 who is neither in work or school) costs taxpayers $14,000 dollars per year. U.S. Government spending is the responsibility and under the control of Congress, which is made up of both Republican and Democratic Party politicians whose primary goal is election and, of course, re-election.

For America to return to a path that leads to prosperity for everyone we have to embrace a philosophy of "value management" that is practiced by astute private businesses to evaluate the cost versus the value (benefit) of every spending program. The enduring value should represent an investment that offers a return that advances our common goals and aspirations to solve the poverty and injustices that currently exist. I believe that the proposed "Apprentice 101" meets these criteria.

CHAPTER 7

The Benefits for Skilled People

Learning and practicing an occupational skill is a life-long attribute that distinguishes an individual and provides personal self-esteem. Every community in the country also benefits from the skilled trades people who are part of the citizenry. Skilled, high income people contribute significantly to the tax base and consumer economy, as well as creating stability within the community. Electricians, plumbers, mechanics, nurses, teachers, or firefighters are indispensable. In America, a skilled trade's person, craftsman, or professional has the potential to become an entrepreneur, be independent, and operate his/her own business with little capital and rely only on their personal skills and knowledge. Any person can register an assumed name, register a business as the principal owner, or form an LLC or corporation and conduct business as an independent contractor. As a business person, they can hire employees, train staff, and legally practice their craft. And millions of American citizens do exactly that. They operate out their home, office, or shop. In America, opportunity is the result of freedom with little or no government involvement. Competent, skilled people have the opportunity to achieve their dreams and direct their economic destiny. Entrepreneurs also benefit in many other ways. For example, a private business person has to develop and demonstrate peripheral skills including leadership, finance, organization and business promotion. The typical business person is very knowledgeable and strives to be a responsible, informed citizen.

A person who chooses to follow a vocational career is not exempt from continuing his or her education as a full or part-time student at any school of higher learning. To the contrary, experiential learning based on work and life experiences enhances a person's chances of completing a college degree at an institution of his or her choice. Skilled people are also in a better financial position to actually afford college tuition without securing a student loan. Many colleges actually offer mature individuals college credit for life-experience. Relatively new trends designed for working adults are the many institutions that offer night and weekend courses to accommodate work and family schedules. Often some of the academic work can be completed via the internet or video-conferencing. In America, advancing one's education and financial aspirations are only a matter of discipline and perseverance.

CHAPTER 8

Entrepreneurs— Business Successes

Jobs are created by entrepreneurs and visionaries who are willing to risk one's fortune to start a new business. Successful businesses are the foundation of our economy. They and their employees perpetuate the American dream by both creating goods and services, as well as consuming the goods and services of other enterprises. They pay the taxes that sustain the government and the country's infrastructure. Below are a few personal examples:

Some Successes

As a professional engineer and CEO of a successful engineering company I would like to share my experience as an owner and observer of start-up companies and job creation. The purpose is to demonstrate that anybody can accomplish extraordinary results, and hopefully inspire readers to follow their dreams and excel in their pursuit of job satisfaction.

1) TEAM Resources, Inc.

In 1989, after 22 years, I resigned my long-time job at General Motors Corporation to become an entrepreneur. I recruited two former GM retirees and my son, a recent graduate with a degree in international business. We formed TEAM (Technical, Engineering, Administrative & Management) Resources, Inc.

We envisioned an American International contract services company to serve the automotive supplier base. Many European and Asian companies were anxious to enter the U.S. market but required American engineering and design expertise. We started TEAM with $ 15,000 seed money. $ 5,000 of that was an advance on my credit card. We hired several recently retired automotive mechanisms designers as our cadre and partnered with a computer service company to provide designer CAD (computer aided design) work-stations. CAD was a relatively new technology which promised increased productivity together with the ability to quickly and efficiently make design revisions, and store the data electronically.

TEAM was successful in acquiring several automotive contracts. CAD operators (formerly draftspersons) were scarce. A shortage of designers with an engineering background existed due to the robust economy at the time. This situation presented an opportunity to recruit and train more CAD employees. We were fortunate to be able to recruit and train a cadre of experienced American engineers in the advanced CAD systems available in the U.S. In order to fulfill our contracts, we recruited European and Asian engineers with advanced degrees (Masters and Ph.Ds.) who were anxious to obtain temporary visas to work in the U.S. The company also registered and licensed TEAM Academy in Michigan to train these recruits in CAD and American design processes. We were successful in gaining prominence with our blended workforce and TEAM Resources, Inc. was selected as one of "Detroit's Future Fifty" companies, three years in a row. Our small firm expanded and we employed over 60 engineers and designers serving the U.S. automotive industry.

2) Meijer, Inc.—1st Hypermarket Store in the United States

Hendrik Meijer, a Dutch immigrant and local barber, founded what became the first "hypermarket" store in the U.S. A "hypermarket", or "supercenter", is a super store that combines groceries and department store goods in the same store. Many Meijer stores also feature a branded gas station combined with a convenience store for fast in-out service. Hendrik and his 14-year-old son Frederik founded the grocery business in 1934 during the Great Depression. Starting with a single store in Greenville, Michigan, the Meijers pioneered the super center store concept and today has 196 superstores throughout the Midwestern United States. At the forefront of customer service innovation, Meijer was among the first store to offer self-service shopping and to provide shopping carts. Half the Meijer stores are in Michigan, but the company has expanded into Illinois, Indiana, Ohio and Kentucky. In 2011 Forbes ranked Meijer's No. 13 on the list of "Americas Largest Private Companies". Entrepreneurs such as Meijer represent the backbone of our economy and job creation.

3) <u>Wild Birds Unlimited</u>

Judith Barrett has always been a lover of nature and an environmental activist. Originally from Royal Oak, Michigan, Judy moved to Traverse City after graduating from Western Michigan University in Kalamazoo, Michigan. As a single mom with an entrepreneurial spirit, Judy's first business venture was selling small bags of feed from the back of her van to visitors, who wanted to feed the ducks and waterfowl, at one of Traverse City's lakeside parks.

A few years later, Judy invested her earnings and savings from the duck feeding business into a relatively new business franchise called "Wild Birds Unlimited". She rented space in a busy shopping center, adjacent to the lakeshore and near the city parks, and opened her original store. Her "Wild Birds Unlimited" has been very successful for over 23 years. Local residents refer to the store as "bird central" and she employs 6 people.

Judith, however, isn't sitting on her laurels. She is venturing into another new business. "Up North Global" is a trendy new "foodie" business that creates and sells gourmet ethnic foods to local stores and at farm markets in Northern Michigan. This business has resulted in a dozen new job opportunities for local cooks and vendors.

Judy Barrett's entrepreneurial spirit has helped invigorate Traverse City and local businesses.

4) <u>Staples, Inc.</u>

    Mitt Romney, in his book "*NO APOLOGY*", describes the establishment of Staples Corporation: "The founder, Tom Stemberg in 1985, had come up with an idea for a new business, one he believed would revolutionize the retail industry, and in particular the business of selling and distributing office supplies. Tom's vision was to create the world's first big-box office products chain, one with hundreds of stores, tens of thousands of employees, and billions in revenues. Most people, I spoke with thought it would never work, but they were wrong, and today Staples is what Tom dreamed it would be.

    "Reaching Tom's goal was difficult. At first the manufacturers of supplies didn't want to sell to him because his idea threatened their traditional distributors. Stores were hard to locate in real-estate-cramped New England where he began. A warehouse with multistore capacity had to be built and financed, even though at first there were only a handful of stores to serve. Copycat competitors sprung up everywhere; at one point, we counted more than a dozen. And money was tight. In the end, because Tom and his team achieved success in the face of so many challenges, Staples and its management team became very strong indeed, and now lead the industry" (Romney, 2010, 21).

    Pursuing a dream in a negative and challenging business and economic environment requires mental courage and discipline that are attributes of an entrepreneur.

CHAPTER 9

Trade and Vocational School Expansion

Apprentice 101 will cause restructuring and expansion of supplemental training/educational institutions. The vocational education industry will adapt to the new opportunities for job and skill enrichment. The increasing number of people entering the job market will result in a reassessment of employment practices and job content formation. Upon graduation, the former apprentices will now be skilled in some craft or occupation. They will be working, and receiving substantial incomes. Their self-worth and confidence will motivate them to do even better. They will have a brighter view of the future and strive to increase their competence and seek higher challenges. Perhaps they will want to expand their horizon and self-train for potential advancement in their current job, or supplement their income by part-time work in their occupation. Many will desire to become entrepreneurs or independent contractors. Achieving his or her dream may require additional skills or training, such as accounting/bookkeeping, management training, new technology, business savvy or other attributes. Many will become leaders, instructors, or teachers, and share their experience and skills to help others.

The result of this natural desire to grow and self-actualize will create an increasing need for the vocational training industry to re-invent itself to offer individualized courses that are unique or specific to an industry or occupation. For example, in the manufacturing industry, the recent increasing competition for quality hatched several new learning techniques. One such innovation known as "Six-Sigma", a procedure based on statistical achievement, results in zero manufacturing defects. In our competitive and constantly-changing world, science and technology continue to advance almost daily. In order to keep up and hopefully excel our workforce must be the best educated. These boutique-type learning opportunities will continue to expand. And this will require more special-skilled people, newest technology, equipment and facilities.

The vocational training industry will become technology leaders, and compete for students with colleges and universities that can't assure employment opportunities to their graduates. Technical oriented and skilled crafts people will be far more likely to secure a good job and have a brighter future than a non-professional college graduate. This competition for young high school graduates may in fact decrease tuition costs, as well as the current demand for student loans and government-sponsored scholarships.

CHAPTER 10

American Education Status

Current Status

The United States was the first nation in history to recognize that public education for every citizen, regardless of class or station, was vital to its future. Since the beginning of our free public education system, we have devoted enormous resources and effort toward enrolling each successive generation in high school and on to college. Today 84 percent of Americans have a high-school diploma. Thirty percent of all Americans are college graduates. Mitt Romney (Romney, 2010, 213) points out that "America's commitment to education helped build a base of human capital that was broader than that of any other nation. That human capital propelled our productivity, which in turn generated higher standards of living, economic growth, and world leadership. Without Americans' collective commitment to education, America would not have reached the heights we have achieved." However, there are ominous signs about where education will take us in the future.

In 1983 the National Commission on Excellence in Education reported "The educational foundations of our society are presently being eroded by a rising tide of mediocrity that threatens our very future as a nation and a people". Now, almost thirty years later, many scholars and researchers are in agreement that we have made virtually no progress in reversing the tide. The National Academy of Sciences has also concluded that America is on a losing path. A recent report commissioned by the Organization for Economic Cooperation and Development ranked American fifteen-year-olds as being 25th in math skills and 21st in science among more than thirty developed nations. After leading the world in public education for most of the twentieth century, we have fallen dramatically below average in the twenty-first century. We still rival other nations in the percentage of students who obtain bachelor degrees, but other countries far surpass us in advanced science and engineering degrees. In 2005, only 6.4 percent of advanced degrees awarded by American universities were in engineering, while in Japan and Korea the percentage was over 30 percent. The commanding lead and global competitive advantage we once had in science and engineering has long since vanished. The consequences for an economy that was once fueled and driven by innovation are ominous.

Education Reform

The current state of our education system is flunking. The popular movie documentary *Waiting for Superman* (Guggenheim, 2010) vividly portrays the failure of our current public education system to provide our young people the knowledge and basic skills necessary to obtain a meaningful job after they graduate from high school. This is especially true for minority and disadvantaged children who have no alternative except for public education. African American and Hispanic American achievement in primary and secondary schools falls far below that of Anglo or Asian American students who actually finish high school. Statistics show that about half of the African American and Hispanic American students drop out before receiving a high school diploma. However, the inexcusable national drop-out rate isn't limited to minorities. Actually, the in absolute numbers, more Anglo students drop out of school than do minorities. Almost 30 percent of all American children do not complete high school. This lack of education virtually assures the creation of a permanent "underclass" (Romney, 2010, 215).

In 2004, President George W. Bush signed the D.C. School Choice Incentive Act of 2003, creating the D.C. Opportunity Scholarship Program, to provide scholarships to low-income families in Washington, D.C. This act established the first federally funded, private school voucher program in the United States and Congress mandated that the program be evaluated for results. Beginning in 2004 the OSP program awarded 1,700 families with $7,500 vouchers per student to help them offset the cost of attending the private schools. The recipients, 99 percent of whom were black or Hispanic enthusiastically endorsed the program, but the disappointment was that there were four applicants for every private school opening. The students who participated in the program developed reading skills that were nineteen months ahead of their public school peers. An evaluation by the Department of Education confirmed that the students had made much progress. However, under intense pressure from opponents of "school choice", the Obama Administration terminated the program in 2009.

Another sad example of "school choice" occurred in Detroit, Michigan. A local philanthropist offered Detroit, through the Michigan legislature, a pledge to personally fund $200 million dollars to establish fifteen charter schools. Unbelievably, the teachers' union successfully persuaded their friends in the Michigan state legislature to turn down the gift. These two experiences in Washington, D.C., and Michigan demonstrate the political forces wielding their enormous power to thwart education reform.

It is an inexplicable human tragedy when millions of American children barely attain a third—world education in the most prosperous nation in the world. Our failure to educate our minority populations is the foremost civil-rights issue of our time. As *Waiting for Superman* documents, teachers' unions supported by politicians, with the approval of federal, state, and local elected officials are "dumbing-down" what was once American educational excellence. There is no greater indictment of American government than the sorry state of American education. It is "criminal" that our government, the U.S. Congress, and elected officials are not willing to reform the American education system that is failing the children as well as the nation's future.

According to John Stossel, "We want to believe that public schools are one of the best parts of America. What reality taught me: government schools are one of the worst parts of America". Stossel also quotes Andrew Coulson, Director of the Center for Educational Freedom, Cato Institute, and a foremost education researcher: "Over the past 40 years, public school employment has risen ten times faster than enrollment" (Stossel, 2012, 190). College tuition has risen 750 percent, and the government has ignored this trend, but instead has attacked business CEO's (job creators), for much smaller increases in their salaries and bonuses. College professors' salaries, benefits, and wasteful spending have a direct impact on student loans and the proliferation of drop-outs, resulting in unemployment and under-employment of young people who also carry high student loan debt.

However, there is much that can be done by the citizenry in spite of the political environment:

- Lobby local school boards to focus on Science, Technology, English and Math (STEM);
- Expand and support "charter schools"; charter schools are better and cheaper than public schools (Stossel, 2012);
- Establish public-financed vocational or trade schools;
- Reward exceptional teachers with significant incentives;
- Offer supplemental tutorial assistance to poverty-prone families & reward them with special incentives if they inspire their children not to drop out of school.
- Council and mentor students about promising higher-paying job opportunities, and
- Solicit entrepreneurs and local businesses to open and broadcast job openings.

Future Educational Trends

Education begins at home. Parents and caregivers are in a unique position to forever influence a child's future. A child views adults as role models and a positive home environment will instill in the child lifelong values, trust and a feeling of serenity.

A concerned parent or caregiver will choose to be involved in their child's education. Interviews with public school teachers revealed that, "If a child's parents come to school on the first day of school or attend parent-teacher meetings, we know that the child will do just fine." (Romney, 2010, 227).

A growing trend in America is the "home-schooling" movement. Concerned parents, who have lost faith in the ability of public schools to properly educate their precious children, are doing it themselves. Hope is eternal, and all American families desire to create a future for their children that is better than theirs. Parents want to be proud of their children and trust our public education system. I believe that Moms especially, want their children to have a promising future and hope that America will deliver their dream. For this to happen there needs to be career opportunities and gainful employment. A good education is essential. Fortunately, we live in a time when emerging technology can circumvent the failed union-dominated public school system.

Cyber Education

Cyber education and innovation are making inroads into self-help, privatized tutorial education. Mitt Romney describes a company called "Advanced Academics" that currently provides classes over the Internet for 60,000 students in twenty-nine states, and each of their courses is supervised by a teacher who federal regulations certify as "highly qualified"(Romney, 2010, 237). There are a number of other companies that also offer various supervised Internet learning. Today, almost one million public school students attend courses online every year. In Dayton, Ohio, children spend several hours online each day in classes that have twice the average number of students and are taught by teachers who receive higher pay for the innovative teaching they do. The state of Wisconsin has chartered a "virtual academy" from a private company that pioneered distance learning. This virtual academy provides a customized curriculum to students who 'attend' from locations all over the state, since their needs were not being met by their own districts. At

Pennsylvania Cyber, the largest "virtual" charter school in the country, where eight thousand students receive textbooks and are assigned individual teachers who work with them online and in real time. A faculty adviser is required to e-mail each student's parents every week and speak with them by phone every two weeks, providing feedback and counseling. The results are impressive—Pennsylvania cyber students have posted SAT scores 97 points above the average for the State.

At least thirty-eight states have now established cyber schools. Florida has the largest enrollment—100,000 students. Students are presented with materials that are tailored to match their capabilities and progress. Teachers monitor each student's progress and advancement, intervening to help guide them through whatever learning challenges arise.

These new technologies also enhance the education experience of home-schooled children. As cyber-tools become even more available, homeschoolers will grow exponentially. The teachers' unions oppose much of this computer-learning revolution because computers can't be organized. Teachers' unions have gone to court to close cyber-schools across the country, including Wisconsin's virtual academy. The concern is that the unions may be successful in blocking technology innovations as they have been in blocking other education reforms through political power. What is needed is leadership at the higher levels of government to free education from the grip of forces that are keeping our schools and our children from realizing their potential.

The American public must keep informed about the status of our educational system. We must insist that politicians don't use this vital issue to enhance their election or re-election hopes by funding their campaigns through donations from selfish special interest groups and lobbyists who don't have the nation's best interest at heart.

CHAPTER 11

College or General Education Pursuit

College Education versus General Education

In America we do not have a national educational occupational training protocol. Instead, our education system is administered by the individual states. People are free to pursue careers as they wish and often wind up in an occupation by chance, opportunity, location or experiential job progression. Many Americans wish to pursue a college education. In America a college degree has become a sign of success to many people.

The college-bound student must have completed high school and have a grade point record and SAT score that meets the entry requirements. Most colleges/universities are selective in who they allow to attend their schools. Typically, colleges/universities have limits on the number of freshman openings that will be available. Therefore entry requirements are intended to restrict the selection of new students to those who have the best grade-point record and/or SAT score. If the applicant's academic transcript is inadequate, he/she must pursue a community college education with lower admission standards, or an alternative career route.

The competition between schools and applicants may be intense for the high qualified candidates. Both the college and the student are seeking some academic or social status to enhance their reputation. This rationing of seats and quest for high potential student applicants results in rising tuition costs.

Higher tuition rates in turn have the unintended consequence of higher student loan commitments. Colleges or universities are perceived as the pinnacle of educational excellence, but this is only true for the "professions": doctors, medical specialists, lawyers, accountants, engineers, teachers, etc. These degrees relate to a specific professional field and typically result in a recognized occupation and social standing. However, most college curriculums are not designed to provide a specific job or occupation upon graduation. Instead they provide the technical and academic experience or tools necessary for the student to pursue a job or position following graduation, at an established business firm. The college graduate is generally hired as a trainee or intern who must go through an extended period of obtaining real-life job experience. While a college education remains the dream of many young people, reliance on a general studies curriculum is not the best path to a successful career.

Recent experience and investigation shows that the college class of 2012 is in for a rude welcome to the world of work. One in two new college graduates are jobless or underemployed. Young adults with bachelor's degrees have to accept lower-wage jobs such as waiter or waitress, bartender, retail clerk or receptionist. Opportunities for college graduates vary widely. While there is a strong demand in science, education and health fields, arts and humanities flounder. According to recent government projections, only three of the 30 occupations with the largest projected number of job openings by 2020 will require a bachelor's degree or higher to fill the position of teachers, college professors and accountants. Most job openings are in professions such as retail sales, fast food and truck driving, jobs which are not easily replaced by computers or technology. College graduates who majored in zoology, anthropology, philosophy art history and humanities were among the least likely to find jobs appropriate to their education level. Those with nursing, teaching, accounting or computer science degrees were among the most likely. Young people entering the workplace should have a predetermined idea as to the type or kind of job they desire or at least the occupational field that interests them. Researching the newspaper or online classified job opening ads is a good way to give the person knowledge of job availability and required education or skills. This probably should be done prior to enrolling in college or other skill training.

In the United States our current fixation on achieving a college degree has led us into a financial abyss. The government's interference with education has resulted in many political and economic confrontations that are threatening our survival as a great nation. Student loans for higher education now exceed *1 trillion dollars*. College students throughout the nation are protesting "Trillion Dollar Day" (Reuters, 2012). Student loan debt now is larger than the total amount of credit card debt or loans for automobiles. Many students cannot repay their loans and sub-prime college loans amount to $ 270 billion. The U. S. government administers the "student loan programs", and is also the beneficiary of both the interest charged (and paid) as well as the loss in revenue due to default. Beginning July 1, 2012, the interest rate on student loans is scheduled to increase from 3.4% to 6.8%, and the profit from the increase will go to pay for "Obama care" and not to student debt reduction or a decrease in tuition. Congress is in a stalemate over this sensitive issue because the interest increase is automatic and part of the "Obama care" fiasco. Neither side agrees as to accept the loss in revenue if the interest rate increase is nullified. In Washington, spending reduction is never a viable option.

An appropriate question is: Should the U. S. government be in the "loan shark" business and exploit young people who are trying to get ahead? Another good question would be: How could the U.S. government reduce the cost of exploding college tuition? College drop-out rate is accelerating, as are both unemployment and under-employment. Our leaders and politicians are in a quandary as to a solution to these serious problems. Meanwhile government handouts and welfare entitlement programs are ballooning every day. Since the government wants to get involved in our young peoples' education they could do it in a positive way. College costs are growing at a much faster rate than the other economic indicators. Congress should examine why this is occurring. Wasteful spending on unnecessary items such as faculty lounges, student entertainment facilities, bloated useless course offerings and a multitude of ancillary services or activities should be curtailed or altogether eliminated. Wasteful college programs and elaborate entertainment facilities that are driving up tuition and student fees, as well as the amount of government sponsored student loans need to be curtailed. Scholarships and grants intended for education are being squandered without any government oversight. Rising tuition and college costs are exacerbating the student loan indebtedness and our government is encouraging this economic disaster for college students.

In summary, a college degree does not equate to a job guarantee. College is a very expensive pursuit that often results in a mediocre career for the hopeful student who graduates with only a Liberal Arts degree and no job experience. More often college students do not graduate at all. Instead, they spend a year or more in school and then drop-out. Often this leaves them with the burden of a student loan that requires repayment. The motivation at this point is to obtain almost any type of meaningful job (Reuters,2012). College is not for everyone, and a country with a preponderance of unemployed college aspirants is not desirable. However, mature college drop-outs can become great candidates for a skilled or business apprenticeship that in fact will result in a fruitful future.

CHAPTER 12

America's Cities and Rural Communities

Across America many citizens of our major cities and rural communities are denied the same employment opportunities that are enjoyed by residents of the more prosperous localities. There are many reasons for the disparity, and most Americans are well aware of the inequities. The list is almost endless but includes the injustices of our political system, social diversity, class envy, regional bigotry, racial and religious division, heritage, etc. These conflicts are precipitated by politicians of both major parties whose primary motivation is to do or say whatever is necessary to assure their elected or appointed positions. The solution to this continuing human tragedy is education and media integrity. An informed and concerned public has the ability to demand refomation of this political and journalistic malfeasance.

The New Deal

Poverty and social disparity has been prevalent in America for many years. Congress has tried to resolve or at least diminish these inequities via political solutions. Beginning in the early 1930's and as a result of the Great Depression, Congress passed legislation designed to rectify the economic inequality that existed between the wealthy and the poor. The "New Deal", introduced by Franklin D. Roosevelt during the 1932 Presidential Campaign was a sincere effort to alleviate the suffering of the disadvantaged as a result of the economic disaster which left millions of Americans unemployed, homeless and hungry. In his acceptance speech, Roosevelt vowed, "I pledge you, I pledge myself, to a new deal for the American people". He further summarized the New Deal as a "use of the authority of government as an organized form of self-help for all classes and groups and sections of our country". The New Deal was consummated by Congress, which passed a variety of economic stimulus bills intended to solve the numerous human and financial problems that were facing the Nation at that time.

The Social Security Act of 1935 was a landmark effort by the U. S. government to reach out in a broad way to alleviate human misery. The Social Security Act and later amendments provide pensions for the aged, benefit payments to dependent mothers, crippled children and blind people, as well as unemployment insurance. This government involvement to help the elderly, poor and unfortunate was a well-intended and earnest initial step toward what today is considered entitlements.

The Great Society

The next major effort by government to rectify economic inequities was the Great Society social reforms promoted by President Lyndon B. Johnson. *The two main goals of the Great Society were the **elimination** of poverty and racial injustice.* The Great society resembled the New Deal domestic agenda, but differed sharply in the types of programs enacted. Unlike the New Deal, which was a response to a severe financial and economic calamity, the Great Society initiatives focused on grave social crises that confronted the nation. The major programs covered were, (1) Civil Rights, (2) War on Poverty, (3) Education, (4) Health, (5) Arts and Culture, (6) Public broadcasting, (7) Transportation, (8) Consumer protection, (9) Environment, and (10) Labor. Much of the Great Society legislation was supported by both Democrat and Republican administrations.

Arthur W. Hoffmann, Ed.D.; P.E.

Civil Rights and the War on Poverty

Racial segregation persisted throughout the South, and in 1964 urban riots broke out in New York City and Los Angeles, followed by hundreds of other cities that experienced major disturbances. The Civil Rights Act was passed by congress in 1964. This act forbade job discrimination and the segregation of public accommodations. In 1965 the Voting Rights Act was implemented to assure minority registration and voting. In 1968, a new Housing Act was passed which banned racial discrimination in housing, and also subsidized the construction or rehabilitation of low-income housing units. In 1968 Congress also approved a new program for federally-funded job retraining for the hardcore unemployed. The most ambitious and controversial part of the Great Society was its initiative to end poverty.

The centerpiece of the War on Poverty was the Economic Opportunity Act of 1964, which created an Office of Economic Opportunity (OEO) to oversee a variety of community-based antipoverty programs. The OEO reflected a consensus among policymakers that the best way to deal with poverty was not simply to raise the incomes of the poor but to help them better themselves through education, job training, and community development.

The War on Poverty spawned dozens of programs, among them the Job Corps, whose purpose was to help disadvantaged youth develop marketable skills; the Neighborhood Youth Corps, established to give poor urban youths work experience and encourage them to stay in school; Volunteers in Service to America (VISTA), domestic version of the Peace Corps, which placed concerned citizens with community-based agencies to work towards empowerment of the poor; the Model Cities Program for urban redevelopment; Upward Bound, which assisted poor high school students entering college; legal services for the poor; the Food Stamp Act of 1964 (which expanded the federal food stamp program); the Community Action Program, which initiated local Community Action Agencies charged with helping the poor become self-sufficient; and Project Head Start, which offered preschool education for poor children. In addition, funding was provided for the establishment of community health centers to expand access to health care, while major amendments were made to Social security in 1965 and 1967 which significantly increased benefits, expanded coverage, and established new programs to combat poverty and raise living standards.

Education Legislation

The Higher Education Act of 1963 (replacing the Land Grant College Bill), provided for college libraries, graduate centers, and technical institutes and classrooms for the expansion of community colleges. The Higher Education Act of 1965 increased federal funding to universities, created scholarships and low-interest loans for students, and established a national Teacher Corps to provide instructors to teach in poverty-stricken areas of the United States. The 1965 Elementary and Secondary Education Act was the most important educational component of the Great Society. Initially this legislation provided funding for the purchase of school materials and the start of special education programs to schools with a high concentration of low-income children. The Act established Head Start as a permanent program.

In 1968 the Bilingual Education Act was passed which offered federal aid to local school districts to assist them to address the needs of children with limited English-speaking ability until it expired in 2002. The 2001 No Child Left Behind Act (NCLB), passed by the George W. Bush Administration is a reauthorization of Elementary and Secondary Education Act. This NCLB Act was due to wide public concern about the state of public education in our country. The NCLB Act expanded the federal role in public education through annual testing, academic progress, report cards, teacher qualifications and funding changes. Education is the "key" ingredient in our recipe for success in defeating poverty.

Arthur W. Hoffmann, Ed.D.; P.E.

Accomplishments of the New Deal and Great Society

Both the New Deal and the Great Society demonstrated what has been the typical sociopolitical response to the critical domestic problems facing America, which were destined to destroy our nation if the government had not acted decisively. In retrospect, opponents and proponents may argue the various actions that both Presidents Roosevelt and Johnson pursued to solve the crises they faced. FDR was faced with the Great Depression he inherited. His response was the New Deal. Lyndon Johnson was confronted with civil unrest, racial inequality, and chronic poverty. Decisive action was necessary, and they acted with good intent. They had the overwhelming support of the electorate and Congress. The results were the economic revival and restoration of civility and growth within our Nation. The immediate crises were resolved, and hope was restored.

However, the core problems of poverty, lack of opportunity, educational deficiencies, and governmental intrusion were not eliminated, and still exist today. What was demonstrated is the ability of the American people to respond with empathy to critical domestic and social problems in order to achieve harmony and progress. The American people expect the government to help solve domestic problems by providing the environment for our free enterprise system to achieve success.

The New Deal and Great Society responded by throwing money, flawed programs and mis-management at problems that require education, training and human behavior modification. What is needed is a more profound understanding of human nature and what is necessary to lift the unfortunate and disadvantaged up from poverty by providing hope and opportunity. Everyone needs to contribute to their own well-being and believe that if they make an effort, they will reap rewards. There has to be a belief that self-help will result in fairness for all and that the American people and our free enterprise system will ensure it.

The Current State of Affairs

After 80 years of entitlement legislation we have made little progress in solving fundamental economic inequalities. A recent Newsmax article presented an overview with statistics related to the War on Poverty. Following is a summary of their news release: "In 1964, when President Lyndon Johnson declared a "war on poverty" in America, the poverty rate stood at around 19 percent. Since then, total federal, state, and local spending on anti-poverty programs has amounted to $ 15 trillion, yet the poverty rate now stands at 15.1 percent, the highest in nearly a decade. Clearly we are doing something wrong."

The Cato Institute has released a new policy analysis on welfare spending that calls the war on poverty a "failure" (Tanner, 2012). "The federal government will spend more than $ 668 billion on anti-poverty programs this year, an increase of 41 percent or more than $ 193 billion since President Barack Obama took office. State and local government expenditures will amount to another $ 284 billion, bringing the total to nearly $ 1 trillion—far more the $ 685 billion spent on defense. Federal, state and local governments now spend $ 20,610 a year for every poor person in the United States, or $ 61,830 for each poor family of three. Given that the poverty line for that family is just $ 18,530, we should have theoretically wiped out poverty many times over".

Most welfare programs are means-tested programs providing cash, food, housing, medical care, or other benefits to low-income persons and families, or targeted at communities or disadvantaged groups, such as the homeless. The U.S. Government alone now funds 126 separate and often overlapping programs designed to fight poverty.

There are 33 separate housing programs run by four different cabinet departments, 21 programs providing food or food purchasing assistance administered by three different federal departments and one independent agency, and eight healthcare programs administered by five separate agencies within the Department of Health and Human Services.

Arthur W. Hoffmann, Ed.D.; P.E.

The largest welfare program is Medicaid, which provides benefits to 49 million Americans and cost more than $ 228 billion last year, followed by the food stamps program, with 41 million participants and a price tag of nearly $ 72 billion. At least 106 million Americans receive benefits from one or more of these programs. The vast majority of current programs are focused on making poverty more comfortable rather than giving people the tools that will help them escape poverty. "What government usually does is make the problem worse and leave us deeper in debt. Why don't we ever learn"? (Stossel, 2012).

It is unfair to blame welfare recipients, who are obviously in need of assistance, for the mis-guided and wasteful government entitlement fiasco that was structured and administered by inept politicians and bureaucrats. The solution to poverty lies with the people themselves and with the assistance of free-market ideas, proper education, and government support for self-help initiatives by knowledgeable practitioners.

CHAPTER 13

A Poverty Solution—
Utilizing Apprentice 101

Apprentice 101 has a special application if we are serious about reducing the chronic poverty in our large cities and rural communities. This introduction and implementation of "apprentice 101" in these critical areas could have a profound effect in reversing the disparity and blight. The jobs creation process is intended to be orchestrated by the people, and for the people, not mandated by any government agency. The basic premise is that the American entrepreneur has the ability and vision to control his or her destiny without governmental interference. Based on the above review of our government's "war on poverty", it is clear that it has been a complete failure.

For over 80 years, taxpayer's money and resources have been squandered as a result of misdirection and mismanagement. Worse than the waste of $15 trillion over four generations, are the destruction of the human spirit and the theft of the dignity and self-esteem of "poor people". For the past four generations, U.S. Government bureaucrats ordained that the destiny of the poor was to remain in poverty. Even the "educational escape route" was blocked by a mediocre public school system. What has been missing in "the war on poverty" is **opportunity,** and freedom to choose. Opportunity (availability) for good jobs, meaningful education, good housing, transportation, role-models (mentors), has not been properly addressed in the fight to eliminate poverty. Past and present programs have only aggravated the poverty situation by trapping the unfortunate who become dependent on unearned entitlements. The political purpose apparently is not to eliminate poverty, but rather to create and maintain a permanent "underclass" that will be indebted to the government for their very existence. The government "anti-poverty" programs are structured to deliver hand-outs, not a helping-hand. To escape poverty requires the utilization of a "boot-straps" philosophy. Practical education, the ("3rs"), personal initiative, opportunity, hope, self-worth, determination, success, and faith in American fairness are all interrelated, and the benefits of a real job's program.

It all begins with **opportunity.** Jobs are the lifeblood of our economic system. Jobs provide the money that pays the employee's salary that in turn generates state and federal tax revenue, consumer spending, savings and investment. The economy also benefits as a result of the labor and services the employee provided. The employee personally benefits by the self-satisfaction that he or she is a useful and productive citizen. Every person desires to be respected by his/her peers and especially if they are recognized and appreciated by the community in which they live. Every community, in turn, values productive citizens. Jobs therefore are a "win-win" outcome for everyone. Within all communities and especially highly populated cities exists a wealth of human resources and capital. Highly skilled people in particular have the wherewithal to share their unique talents and knowledge with the younger generation. This mentoring is in fact a natural phenomenon that breeds respect and admiration for both mentor and student. This dissemination of experience is a valuable asset that needs to be promoted by community leaders.

The job opportunities are generated by the businesses and skilled citizens who volunteer and are willing to hire a young person who will become an asset to both them and our country.

Hopefully, these "apprenticeship" candidates will be selected from the central cities and communities that are in need of business expansion. Businesses and organizations that are located in high population areas have an implied obligation to hire local residents to fill job opening opportunities. This would represent real "justice" by offering opportunities to the less fortunate. Creating good jobs for inner city residents would expedite the flight out-of-poverty. It is likely, in densely populated areas to find small businesses, skilled trades and crafts persons who are willing to offer employment opportunities to the youths in their neighborhood. Local businesses and experienced neighbors with trainable skills can make a real contribution to achieve social justice. Just the fact that job opportunities are available is an incentive for young people to excel in school and strive for a good job. Parents and families in high unemployment areas need to have hope for their children's future. Good job opportunities are the essential resource to fight poverty. The "apprenticeship" route is a promising method for expediting the transition from poverty to prosperity. We must also recognize and offer returning veterans an opportunity for entrance into an apprenticeship job. Soldier-heroes pay an enormous price to ensure our future, and we have an obligation to ensure their future as well.

CHAPTER 14

Endnote

The proposed "jobs initiative" is not intended to be exclusively for highly skilled occupations, although they are eminently desirable. All job occupations qualify for consideration, since any new job inherently adds to the economy and results in another taxpaying citizen and Social Security participant. "Apprentice 101" is a proposed jobs initiative that is voluntary, unstructured, and not a government-regulated program. Private individuals, small or large businesses, trade organizations, unions, municipalities, etc. can offer to sponsor a candidate of their choice, and receive a generous tax credit (provided that Congress approves this type of employer stipend in the IRS rules). The government-authorized tax credit incentive is actually an investment in America that promises to be extraordinary.

"According to researchers from Columbia University and the City University of New York, each unemployed youth—someone between the ages of 16 and 24 who is in neither work or school—costs taxpayers nearly $14,000 dollars per year in direct costs for things like medical bills and government aid, while ultimately creating a "social burden" of more than $37,000 dollars annually (when accounting for the costs of crime and lost tax revenue)." Our current generation of unemployed youth "will cost taxpayers $437 billion dollars over the next five years, and $1.15 trillion dollars over the course of their lifetime" (Garofalo, 2012).

"Apprentice 101" is a specific idea that allows American citizens to influence the destiny of our Nation. Citizenship requires responsibility and empathy for others who may need a helping hand to experience the American dream. All entrepreneurs and business owners owe a measure of gratitude to America for their fortuitous positions, and many are willing to share their knowledge and experience to assure the next generation of Americans will also excel.

Our politicians, both Republican and Democrat, have failed America. While America remains the greatest nation on Earth, we are fast losing our dominant position. We are a nation that has everything, educated people (a melting pot of nationalities, race and religions), with abundant natural resources and totally self-reliant. Our country is geographically isolated from most of the rest of the world and safe from a threat of exterior invasion. However, we find ourselves deep in debt (especially to foreign nations), and our citizens economically divided. This is especially the case in our major cities and rural communities where poverty is most common. Our political divide has resulted in squandering our wealth to satisfy the constituents of both parties. The war on poverty continues and the recipients are at risk of becoming a permanent "underclass". The opposite is true of the wasted wealth that has been squandered to try to bail out the financial institutions and markets that control the monetary wealth of the country. Taxpayers are the people who are paying for this political failure and lack of constructive solutions. The result is the potential demise of America and the destruction of the once prosperous middle class. Only general philosophical solutions are offered by our politicians to improve the economy: (see Appendix for alternative suggestions for job and economic growth):

(1) Democrats: Tax the rich and spread the wealth, and
(2) Republicans: Stop the hand-outs and get a job.

The rich already pay most of the taxes and they also generate more new wealth and revenue (Stossel, 2012). Higher taxes on the rich doesn't equate to more income and benefits and wealth for the poor. The solution is to expand the middle-class. Create job opportunities for young people to move up into the middle-class. To do so, we must create good-paying jobs for everyone, but especially the poor and unfortunate. Apprentice 101 would be a great start.

Epilogue

Author's Comments

I was born in Detroit, Michigan in 1936. My early formative years (1940 to 1960) were very interesting, and covered the transitional period from the outbreak of World War II thru the brief interim peace period (1946 to 1950) prior to the Korean Conflict and on thru the memorable Fifties. Growing up in a major American city like Detroit has fond memories. Detroit was the automobile manufacturing center of the world. Manufacturing attracted many workers from the southern states, as well as many immigrants. During World War II, Detroit became the "arsenal of democracy" as auto manufacturing transitioned to design and production of military vehicles and bombers. Attending school during this period was a lot different than it is today. During the "war", patriotism was foremost. Everyone sacrificed, and gas for cars was rationed as was rubber, sugar, and scarce war materials. There was for, the first time, a short period of civil unrest in the early forties. For our purpose, the education system is of interest. There were many trade and vocational schools that offered courses in machine shop, drafting, and auto mechanics. Science and basic math were essential. Memorizing the multiplication tables was actually required. College prep curriculums were only offered to a selected few. All students were ranked and categorized for future potential. The choice of school in which to enroll was primarily determined by the neighborhood in which you lived. In the cities there was no bussing. Students either walked to school or boarded public busses or the trolley. Disruptive or undisciplined students were sent to reform schools where shop or manual labor skills were taught.

Arthur W. Hoffmann, Ed.D.; P.E.

There were highly recognized trade and vocational schools which required entrance requirements because of a shortage of experienced skilled instructors. The graduates of these schools were in high demand. In Detroit we had schools with national reputations. For example, Detroit's Cass Technical High School was universally known, as was Murray-Wright, and certainly Henry Ford Trade School, which I attended. Graduates automatically were given apprenticeships and were paid a stipend. Competition for these graduates was fierce and the company sponsored schools were privatized and eventually closed, or the enrollment rationed and controlled to prevent predatory raiding of the graduate students.

It was a time in our history when everyone considered a skilled trades-person with respect and admiration. It was this work and dedication that established the American middle-class, that today is being exploited and demeaned by many politicians and their party affiliation.

The purpose of this book is to inspire Americans to return to our roots to ensure that our heritage is not destroyed by a government that defiles our history and resents individual freedom.

Please keep America free for future generations! AWH.

Communication and Contact Protocal

The author has registered a domain name and established a website for interested parties to comment, suggest or support the "jobs initiative" outlined in this book. It would be helpful if proponents would contact their elected representatives and encourage them to support this grass-roots effort to re-direct America.

For more info: **www.apprentice101.com**

APPENDIX

APPENDIX

APPENDIX A

Other Suggestions for Job and Economic Growth

In the course of my research for this book I was exposed to many economic stimulus ideas that politicians, leaders, and business/financial managers have proposed as potential solutions to our Nation's unemployment and economic downturn. However, there is not universal agreement of the various ideas because some are in conflict with each other and represent the differing philosophy of the two political parties. Other ideas are considered self-serving and represent competing factions of the economic plight. There is general agreement that economic growth implies job growth for the country. The following is a list of the primary proposals that have been suggested as a means to improve our economic growth:

(1) Tax reduction is always at the top of the list. Usually, the reference is toward tax rates for businesses or individuals or both. It becomes very complex since deductions, credits, exemptions, and special inducements that result in unintended consequences and gridlock;

(2) Tax increases on various segments of the economy are a popular alternative to tax reduction. This philosophy is rooted in class-envy or competing interests also resulting in gridlock;

(3) More government regulation or less regulation is often a leading option to enhance economic output;

(4) Reduce government waste, and spending/debt are often mentioned;
(5) Employers not hiring due to cost implications of Obama care;
(6) Concern for inflation and U.S. dollar devaluation;
(7) Cost of ongoing wars in faraway places;
(8) High energy cost and dependence on foreign oil;
(9) Illegals are filling American jobs, including skilled building trades; and
(10) Manufacturing out-sourced & companies need incentives to reverse process.

One interesting proposal was advanced by former President Clinton, *Back to Work*, "fill 3 million open jobs that require skilled workers. Employers need to train on the job." Across America there is a shortage of skilled people, especially in science, engineering, and technology jobs that require math or unique knowledge. The "Apprentice101" program would be an ideal solution to help fill many of these open positions directly.

The basic problem with many of the above suggestions for improving the job market (more jobs, better jobs, and viable candidates), is that in order to accomplish the goal, Congressional approval is required. The past and current "gridlock", has to be resolved by the politicians of both parties if America is to remain "that shining city on a hill" (Ronald Reagan).

APPENDIX B

Carpenter Joe
Without Apprentice Tax Credit

Page 1

Form 1040 Department of the Treasury—Internal Revenue Service (99)
U.S. Individual Income Tax Return 2011   OMB No. 1545-0074   IRS Use Only—Do not write or staple in this space.

For the year Jan. 1–Dec. 31, 2011, or other tax year beginning _____, 2011, ending _____, 20 _____   See separate instructions.

Your first name and initial: JOE	Last name: CARPENTER
Your social security number: 012-34-5678	
If a joint return, spouse's first name and initial: MARY	Last name: CARPENTER
Spouse's social security number: 123-45-6789	
Home address (number and street): 12345 MAIN STREET	Apt. no.
City, town or post office, state, and ZIP code: ANYTOWN MI 01234	

Make sure the SSN(s) above and on line 6c are correct.

Presidential Election Campaign — Check here if you, or your spouse if filing jointly, want $3 to go to this fund. Checking a box below will not change your tax or refund. ☐ You ☐ Spouse

Filing Status (Check only one box.)
1. ☐ Single
2. ☒ Married filing jointly (even if only one had income)
3. ☐ Married filing separately. Enter spouse's SSN above and full name here. ▶
4. ☐ Head of household (with qualifying person). (See instructions.) If the qualifying person is a child but not your dependent, enter this child's name here. ▶
5. ☐ Qualifying widow(er) with dependent child

Exemptions
- 6a ☒ Yourself. If someone can claim you as a dependent, do not check box 6a . . .
- b ☒ Spouse . . . .
- c Dependents:
  - (1) First name Last name
  - (2) Dependent's social security number
  - (3) Dependent's relationship to you
  - (4) ✓ if child under age 17 qualifying for child tax credit (see instructions)

Boxes checked on 6a and 6b: **2**
No. of children on 6c who:
• lived with you
• did not live with you due to divorce or separation (see instructions)
Dependents on 6c not entered above
Add numbers on lines above ▶ **2**

If more than four dependents, see instructions and check here ▶ ☐

d Total number of exemptions claimed . . . .

Income

Attach Form(s) W-2 here. Also attach Forms W-2G and 1099-R if tax was withheld.

If you did not get a W-2, see instructions.

Enclose, but do not attach, any payment. Also, please use Form 1040-V.

7	Wages, salaries, tips, etc. Attach Form(s) W-2	
8a	Taxable interest. Attach Schedule B if required	
8b	Tax-exempt interest. Do not include on line 8a	
9a	Ordinary dividends. Attach Schedule B if required	
9b	Qualified dividends	
10	Taxable refunds, credits, or offsets of state and local income taxes	
11	Alimony received	
12	Business income or (loss). Attach Schedule C or C-EZ	69,858.
13	Capital gain or (loss). Attach Schedule D if required. If not required, check here ▶ ☐	
14	Other gains or (losses). Attach Form 4797	
15a	IRA distributions 15a b Taxable amount	15b
16a	Pensions and annuities 16a b Taxable amount	16b
17	Rental real estate, royalties, partnerships, S corporations, trusts, etc. Attach Schedule E	
18	Farm income or (loss). Attach Schedule F	
19	Unemployment compensation	
20a	Social security benefits 20a b Taxable amount	20b
21	Other income. List type and amount _____	
22	Combine the amounts in the far right column for lines 7 through 21. This is your **total income** ▶	69,858.

Adjusted Gross Income

23	Educator expenses	
24	Certain business expenses of reservists, performing artists, and fee-basis government officials. Attach Form 2106 or 2106-EZ	
25	Health savings account deduction. Attach Form 8889	
26	Moving expenses. Attach Form 3903	
27	Deductible part of self-employment tax. Attach Schedule SE	4,934.
28	Self-employed SEP, SIMPLE, and qualified plans	
29	Self-employed health insurance deduction	
30	Penalty on early withdrawal of savings	
31a	Alimony paid b Recipient's SSN ▶	
32	IRA deduction	
33	Student loan interest deduction	
34	Tuition and fees. Attach Form 8917	
35	Domestic production activities deduction. Attach Form 8903	
36	Add lines 23 through 35	4,934.
37	Subtract line 36 from line 22. This is your **adjusted gross income** ▶	64,924.

For Disclosure, Privacy Act, and Paperwork Reduction Act Notice, see separate instructions.   BAA   REV 02/22/12 TTW   Form **1040** (2011)

Carpenter Joe
Without Apprentice Tax Credit

Form 1040 (2011) — Page 2

Tax and Credits	38	Amount from line 37 (adjusted gross income)	38	64,924.
	39a	Check { ☐ You were born before January 2, 1947, ☐ Blind. } Total boxes if: { ☐ Spouse was born before January 2, 1947, ☐ Blind. } checked ▶ 39a		
Standard Deduction for—	b	If your spouse itemizes on a separate return or you were a dual-status alien, check here ▶ 39b ☐		
• People who check any box on line 39a or 39b or who can be claimed as a dependent, see instructions.	40	**Itemized deductions** (from Schedule A) or your **standard deduction** (see left margin)	40	11,600.
	41	Subtract line 40 from line 38	41	53,324.
	42	**Exemptions.** Multiply $3,700 by the number on line 6d	42	7,400.
	43	**Taxable income.** Subtract line 42 from line 41. If line 42 is more than line 41, enter -0-	43	45,924.
	44	**Tax** (see instructions). Check if any from: a ☐ Form(s) 8814 b ☐ Form 4972 c ☐ 962 election	44	6,039.
• All others:	45	**Alternative minimum tax** (see instructions). Attach Form 6251	45	
Single or Married filing separately, $5,800	46	Add lines 44 and 45 ▶	46	6,039.
	47	Foreign tax credit. Attach Form 1116 if required	47	
Married filing jointly or Qualifying widow(er), $11,600	48	Credit for child and dependent care expenses. Attach Form 2441	48	
	49	Education credits from Form 8863, line 23	49	
	50	Retirement savings contributions credit. Attach Form 8880	50	
Head of household, $8,500	51	Child tax credit (see instructions)	51	
	52	Residential energy credits. Attach Form 5695	52	
	53	Other credits from Form: a ☐ 3800 b ☐ 8801 c ☐	53	
	54	Add lines 47 through 53. These are your **total credits**	54	
	55	Subtract line 54 from line 46. If line 54 is more than line 46, enter -0- ▶	55	6,039.
Other Taxes	56	Self-employment tax. Attach Schedule SE	56	8,580.
	57	Unreported social security and Medicare tax from Form: a ☐ 4137 b ☐ 8919	57	
	58	Additional tax on IRAs, other qualified retirement plans, etc. Attach Form 5329 if required	58	
	59a	Household employment taxes from Schedule H	59a	
	b	First-time homebuyer credit repayment. Attach Form 5405 if required	59b	
	60	Other taxes. Enter code(s) from instructions _____	60	
	61	Add lines 55 through 60. This is your **total tax** ▶	61	14,619.
Payments	62	Federal income tax withheld from Forms W-2 and 1099	62	
	63	2011 estimated tax payments and amount applied from 2010 return	63	
If you have a qualifying child, attach Schedule EIC.	64a	**Earned income credit (EIC)**	64a	
	b	Nontaxable combat pay election	64b	
	65	Additional child tax credit. Attach Form 8812	65	
	66	American opportunity credit from Form 8863, line 14	66	
	67	First-time homebuyer credit from Form 5405, line 10	67	
	68	Amount paid with request for extension to file	68	
	69	Excess social security and tier 1 RRTA tax withheld	69	
	70	Credit for federal tax on fuels. Attach Form 4136	70	
	71	Credits from Form: a ☐ 2439 b ☐ 8839 c ☐ 8801 d ☐ 8885	71	
	72	Add lines 62, 63, 64a, and 65 through 71. These are your **total payments** ▶	72	
Refund	73	If line 72 is more than line 61, subtract line 61 from line 72. This is the amount you **overpaid**	73	
	74a	Amount of line 73 you want **refunded to you.** If Form 8888 is attached, check here ▶ ☐	74a	
Direct deposit? See instructions.	b	Routing number XXXXXXXXX ▶ c Type: ☐ Checking ☐ Savings		
	d	Account number XXXXXXXXXXXXXXXXX		
	75	Amount of line 73 you want applied to your 2012 estimated tax ▶ 75		
Amount You Owe	76	**Amount you owe.** Subtract line 72 from line 61. For details on how to pay, see instructions ▶	76	14,619.
	77	Estimated tax penalty (see instructions) 77		

Third Party Designee — Do you want to allow another person to discuss this return with the IRS (see instructions)? ☐ Yes.
Designee's name ▶   Phone no. ▶   Personal identification number (PIN) ▶

No Tax Credit

Sign Here
Under penalties of perjury, I declare that I have examined this return and accompanying schedules and statements, and to the best of my knowledge and belief, they are true, correct, and complete. Declaration of preparer (other than taxpayer) is based on all information of which preparer has any knowledge.

Joint return? See instructions. Keep a copy for your records.

Your signature   Date   Your occupation: CARPENTER   Daytime phone number: (888) 888-8888
Spouse's signature. If a joint return, **both** must sign.   Date   Spouse's occupation: SELF-EMPLOYED   If the IRS sent you an Identity Protection PIN, enter it here (see inst.)

Paid Preparer Use Only
Print/Type preparer's name   Preparer's signature   Date   Check ☐ if self-employed   PTIN
Firm's name ▶ SELF PREPARED   Firm's EIN ▶
Firm's address ▶   Phone no.

REV 02/22/12 TTW

Form **1040** (2011)

Carpenter Joe
With Apprentice Tax Credit
Page 2

Form 1040 (2011)

Line	Description	Amount
38	Amount from line 37 (adjusted gross income)	64,924.
39a	Check: ☐ You were born before January 2, 1947, ☐ Blind. ☐ Spouse was born before January 2, 1947, ☐ Blind. Total boxes checked ▶ 39a ☐	
39b	If your spouse itemizes on a separate return or you were a dual-status alien, check here ▶ 39b ☐	

Tax and Credits

Standard Deduction for—
- People who check any box on line 39a or 39b or who can be claimed as a dependent, see instructions.
- All others:
  Single or Married filing separately, $5,800
  Married filing jointly or Qualifying widow(er), $11,600
  Head of household, $8,500

Line	Description	Amount
40	Itemized deductions (from Schedule A) or your standard deduction (see left margin)	11,600.
41	Subtract line 40 from line 38	53,324.
42	Exemptions. Multiply $3,700 by the number on line 6d	7,400.
43	Taxable income. Subtract line 42 from line 41. If line 42 is more than line 41, enter -0-	45,924.
44	Tax (see instructions). Check if any from: a ☐ Form(s) 8814 b ☐ Form 4972 c ☐ 962 election	6,039.
45	Alternative minimum tax (see instructions). Attach Form 6251	
46	Add lines 44 and 45 ▶	6,039.
47	Foreign tax credit. Attach Form 1116 if required	
48	Credit for child and dependent care expenses. Attach Form 2441	
49	Education credits from Form 8863, line 23	
50	Retirement savings contributions credit. Attach Form 8880	
51	Child tax credit (see instructions)	
52	Residential energy credits. Attach Form 5695	
53	Other credits from Form: a ☐ 3800 b ☐ 8801 c ☐	
54	Add lines 47 through 53. These are your total credits	
55	Subtract line 54 from line 46. If line 54 is more than line 46, enter -0- ▶	6,039.

Other Taxes

Line	Description	Amount
56	Self-employment tax. Attach Schedule SE	8,580.
57	Unreported social security and Medicare tax from Form: a ☐ 4137 b ☐ 8919	
58	Additional tax on IRAs, other qualified retirement plans, etc. Attach Form 5329 if required	
59a	Household employment taxes from Schedule H	
59b	First-time homebuyer credit repayment. Attach Form 5405 if required	
60	Other taxes. Enter code(s) from instructions	
61	Add lines 55 through 60. This is your total tax ▶	14,619.

Payments

If you have a qualifying child, attach Schedule EIC.

Line	Description	Amount
62	Federal income tax withheld from Forms W-2 and 1099	
63	2011 estimated tax payments and amount applied from 2010 return	
64a	Earned income credit (EIC)	
64b	Nontaxable combat pay election 64b	
65	Additional child tax credit. Attach Form 8812	
66	American opportunity credit from Form 8863, line 14	14,000.
67	First-time homebuyer credit from Form 5405, line 10	
68	Amount paid with request for extension to file	
69	Excess social security and tier 1 RRTA tax withheld	
70	Credit for federal tax on fuels. Attach Form 4136	
71	Credits from Form: a ☐ 2439 b ☐ 8839 c ☐ 8801 d ☐ 8885	
72	Add lines 62, 63, 64a, and 65 through 71. These are your total payments ▶	14,000.

Refund

Direct deposit? See instructions.

Line	Description	Amount
73	If line 72 is more than line 61, subtract line 61 from line 72. This is the amount you overpaid	
74a	Amount of line 73 you want refunded to you. If Form 8888 is attached, check here ▶ ☐	
b	Routing number XXXXXXXXX ▶ c Type: ☐ Checking ☐ Savings	
d	Account number XXXXXXXXXXXXXXXXX	
75	Amount of line 73 you want applied to your 2012 estimated tax ▶ 75	

Amount You Owe

Line	Description	Amount
76	Amount you owe. Subtract line 61 from line 72. For details on how to pay, see instructions ▶	619.
77	Estimated tax penalty (see instructions) 77	

Third Party Designee

Do you want to allow another person to discuss this return with the IRS (see instructions)? ☐ Yes

With Tax Credit

Designee's name ▶   Phone no. ▶   Personal identification number (PIN) ▶

Sign Here

Under penalties of perjury, I declare that I have examined this return and accompanying schedules and statements, and to the best of my knowledge and belief, they are true, correct, and complete. Declaration of preparer (other than taxpayer) is based on all information of which preparer has any knowledge.

Joint return? See instructions.
Keep a copy for your records.

Your signature | Date | Your occupation: CARPENTER | Daytime phone number: (888) 888-8888
Spouse's signature. If a joint return, both must sign. | Date | Spouse's occupation: SELF-EMPLOYED | If the IRS sent you an Identity Protection PIN, enter it here (see inst.)

Paid Preparer Use Only

Print/Type preparer's name | Preparer's signature | Date | Check ☐ if self-employed | PTIN
Firm's name ▶ SELF PREPARED | Firm's EIN ▶
Firm's address ▶ | Phone no.

REV 02/22/12 TTW

Form 1040 (2011)

Carpenter Joe
Without Apprentice Tax Credit
Page 3

SCHEDULE C
(Form 1040)
Department of the Treasury
Internal Revenue Service (99)

Profit or Loss From Business
(Sole Proprietorship)

► For information on Schedule C and its instructions, go to www.irs.gov/schedulec
► Attach to Form 1040, 1040NR, or 1041; partnerships generally must file Form 1065.

OMB No. 1545-0074

2011

Attachment Sequence No. **09**

Name of proprietor: **JOE CARPENTER**
Social security number (SSN): **012-34-5678**

A	Principal business or profession, including product or service (see instructions) **CARPENTRY**	B	Enter code from instructions ► 2 3 8 3 5 0
C	Business name. If no separate business name, leave blank.	D	Employer ID number (EIN), (see instr.) 3 8 1 2 3 4 5 6 7
E	Business address (including suite or room no.) ► **12345 MAIN STREET** City, town or post office, state, and ZIP code **ANYTOWN, MI 01234**		
F	Accounting method: (1) ☒ Cash (2) ☐ Accrual (3) ☐ Other (specify) ►		
G	Did you "materially participate" in the operation of this business during 2011? If "No," see instructions for limit on losses . . ☒ Yes ☐ No		
H	If you started or acquired this business during 2011, check here . . . . ► ☐		
I	Did you make any payments in 2011 that would require you to file Form(s) 1099? (see instructions) . . . . ☐ Yes ☒ No		
J	If "Yes," did you or will you file all required Forms 1099? . . . . ☐ Yes ☐ No

Part I — Income

1a	Merchant card and third party payments. For 2011, enter -0- . . .	1a	0.	
b	Gross receipts or sales not entered on line 1a (see instructions) . .	1b	100,000.	
c	Income reported to you on Form W-2 if the "Statutory Employee" box on that form was checked. **Caution.** See instr. before completing this line	1c		
d	**Total gross receipts.** Add lines 1a through 1c		1d	100,000.
2	Returns and allowances plus any other adjustments (see instructions)		2	
3	Subtract line 2 from line 1d		3	100,000.
4	Cost of goods sold (from line 42)		4	
5	**Gross profit.** Subtract line 4 from line 3		5	100,000.
6	Other income, including federal and state gasoline or fuel tax credit or refund (see instructions) . .		6	
7	**Gross income.** Add lines 5 and 6 . . . . ►		7	100,000.

Part II — Expenses Enter expenses for business use of your home only on line 30.

8	Advertising	8		18	Office expense (see instructions)	18
9	Car and truck expenses (see instructions)	9		19	Pension and profit-sharing plans .	19
10	Commissions and fees .	10		20	Rent or lease (see instructions):	
11	Contract labor (see instructions)	11		a	Vehicles, machinery, and equipment	20a
12	Depletion	12		b	Other business property . . .	20b
13	Depreciation and section 179 expense deduction (not included in Part III) (see instructions)	13		21	Repairs and maintenance . . .	21
				22	Supplies (not included in Part III)	22
				23	Taxes and licenses	23	2,142.
				24	Travel, meals, and entertainment:	
14	Employee benefit programs (other than on line 19) . .	14		a	Travel	24a
15	Insurance (other than health)	15		b	Deductible meals and entertainment (see instructions)	24b
16	Interest:			25	Utilities	25
a	Mortgage (paid to banks, etc.)	16a		26	Wages (less employment credits) .	26
b	Other	16b		27a	Other expenses (from line 48) . .	27a	28,000.
17	Legal and professional services	17		b	Reserved for future use . . .	27b
28	Total expenses before expenses for business use of home. Add lines 8 through 27a . . . . . . ►		28	30,142.
29	Tentative profit or (loss). Subtract line 28 from line 7		29	69,858.
30	Expenses for business use of your home. Attach **Form 8829.** Do not report such expenses elsewhere . .		30	
31	**Net profit or (loss).** Subtract line 30 from line 29.			
	• If a profit, enter on both **Form 1040, line 12** (or **Form 1040NR, line 13**) and on **Schedule SE, line 2.** If you entered an amount on line 1c, see instr. Estates and trusts, enter on **Form 1041, line 3.**		31	69,858.
	• If a loss, you **must** go to line 32.			
32	If you have a loss, check the box that describes your investment in this activity (see instructions).			
	• If you checked 32a, enter the loss on both **Form 1040, line 12,** (or **Form 1040NR, line 13**) and on **Schedule SE, line 2.** If you entered an amount on line 1c, see the instructions for line 31. Estates and trusts, enter on **Form 1041, line 3.**	32a ☐ All investment is at risk. 32b ☐ Some investment is not at risk.		
	• If you checked 32b, you **must** attach **Form 6198.** Your loss may be limited.			

For Paperwork Reduction Act Notice, see your tax return instructions. REV 01/11/12 TTW

Carpenter Joe
Without Apprentice Tax Credit

Schedule C (Form 1040) 2011   Page 4

Part III   Cost of Goods Sold (see instructions)

33 Method(s) used to value closing inventory: a ☐ Cost   b ☐ Lower of cost or market   c ☐ Other (attach explanation)

34 Was there any change in determining quantities, costs, or valuations between opening and closing inventory?
If "Yes," attach explanation . . . . ☐ Yes   ☐ No

35 Inventory at beginning of year. If different from last year's closing inventory, attach explanation . . .	35	
36 Purchases less cost of items withdrawn for personal use	36	
37 Cost of labor. Do not include any amounts paid to yourself	37	
38 Materials and supplies	38	
39 Other costs	39	
40 Add lines 35 through 39	40	
41 Inventory at end of year	41	
42 Cost of goods sold. Subtract line 41 from line 40. Enter the result here and on line 4	42	

Part IV   Information on Your Vehicle. Complete this part only if you are claiming car or truck expenses on line 9 and are not required to file Form 4562 for this business. See the instructions for line 13 to find out if you must file Form 4562.

43 When did you place your vehicle in service for business purposes? (month, day, year) ▶ _____

44 Of the total number of miles you drove your vehicle during 2011, enter the number of miles you used your vehicle for:

a Business _____   b Commuting (see instructions) _____   c Other _____

45 Was your vehicle available for personal use during off-duty hours? . . . . ☐ Yes   ☐ No

46 Do you (or your spouse) have another vehicle available for personal use? . . . . ☐ Yes   ☐ No

47a Do you have evidence to support your deduction? . . . . ☐ Yes   ☐ No

b If "Yes," is the evidence written? . . . . ☐ Yes   ☐ No

Part V   Other Expenses. List below business expenses not included on lines 8–26 or line 30.

WAGES - TOM	28,000.
48 Total other expenses. Enter here and on line 27a	**48**	**28,000.**

REV 01/11/12 TTW   Schedule C (Form 1040) 2011

Carpenter Joe
Without Apprentice Tax Credit
Page 5

SCHEDULE SE
(Form 1040)

Department of the Treasury
Internal Revenue Service (99)

► Attach to Form 1040 or Form 1040NR. ► See separate instructions.

Self-Employment Tax

OMB No. 1545-0074

2011

Attachment Sequence No. **17**

Name of person with **self-employment** income (as shown on Form 1040)
JOE CARPENTER

Social security number of person
with self-employment income ► 012-34-5678

Before you begin: To determine if you must file Schedule SE, see the instructions.

May I Use Short Schedule SE or Must I Use Long Schedule SE?

Note. Use this flowchart **only** if you must file Schedule SE. If unsure, see *Who Must File Schedule SE* in the instructions.

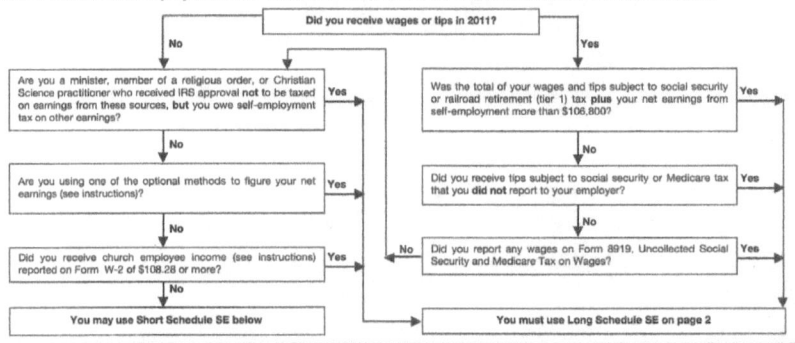

Section A—Short Schedule SE. Caution. Read above to see if you can use Short Schedule SE.

1a	Net farm profit or (loss) from Schedule F, line 34, and farm partnerships, Schedule K-1 (Form 1065), box 14, code A	1a	
b	If you received social security retirement or disability benefits, enter the amount of Conservation Reserve Program payments included on Schedule F, line 4b, or listed on Schedule K-1 (Form 1065), box 20, code Y	1b	( )
2	Net profit or (loss) from Schedule C, line 31; Schedule C-EZ, line 3; Schedule K-1 (Form 1065), box 14, code A (other than farming); and Schedule K-1 (Form 1065-B), box 9, code J1. Ministers and members of religious orders, see instructions for types of income to report on this line. See instructions for other income to report	2	69,858.
3	Combine lines 1a, 1b, and 2	3	69,858.
4	Multiply line 3 by 92.35% (.9235). If less than $400, you do not owe self-employment tax; do not file this schedule unless you have an amount on line 1b . . . . ►	4	64,514.
	Note. If line 4 is less than $400 due to Conservation Reserve Program payments on line 1b, see instructions.		
5	Self-employment tax. If the amount on line 4 is: • $106,800 or less, multiply line 4 by 13.3% (.133). Enter the result here and on **Form 1040, line 56**, or **Form 1040NR, line 54** • More than $106,800, multiply line 4 by 2.9% (.029). Then, add $11,107.20 to the result. Enter the total here and on **Form 1040, line 56**, or **Form 1040NR, line 54**	5	8,580.
6	Deduction for employer-equivalent portion of self-employment tax. If the amount on line 5 is: • $14,204.40 or less, multiply line 5 by 57.51% (.5751) • More than $14,204.40, multiply line 5 by 50% (.50) and add $1,067 to the result. Enter the result here and on **Form 1040, line 27**, or **Form 1040NR, line 27**	6	4,934.

For Paperwork Reduction Act Notice, see your tax return instructions.

REV 12/01/11 TTW

Apprentice Tom
Pays Income Tax & Social Security / Medicare

Page 1

Form **1040A** Department of the Treasury—Internal Revenue Service
U.S. Individual Income Tax Return (99) **2011** IRS Use Only—Do not write or staple in this space.

OMB No. 1545-0074

Your first name and initial	Last name	Your social security number
TOM	APPRENTICE	234-56-7890

If a joint return, spouse's first name and initial | Last name | Spouse's social security number

Home address (number and street). If you have a P.O. box, see instructions. | Apt. no.
13579 OAK STREET

▲ Make sure the SSN(s) above and on line 6c are correct.

City, town or post office, state, and ZIP code. If you have a foreign address, also complete spaces below (see instructions).
ANYTOWN MI 01234

Foreign country name | Foreign province/county | Foreign postal code

Presidential Election Campaign
Check here if you, or your spouse if filing jointly, want $3 to go to this fund. Checking a box below will not change your tax or refund. ☐ You ☐ Spouse

Filing status
Check only one box.
1 ☒ Single
2 ☐ Married filing jointly (even if only one had income)
3 ☐ Married filing separately. Enter spouse's SSN above and full name here. ▶
4 ☐ Head of household (with qualifying person). (See instructions.) If the qualifying person is a child but not your dependent, enter this child's name here. ▶
5 ☐ Qualifying widow(er) with dependent child (see instructions)

Exemptions
6a ☒ **Yourself.** If someone can claim you as a dependent, **do not** check box 6a.
b ☐ **Spouse**

Boxes checked on 6a and 6b **1**
No. of children on 6c who:
• lived with you
• did not live with you due to divorce or separation (see instructions)
Dependents on 6c not entered above

c **Dependents:**

(1) First name Last name	(2) Dependent's social security number	(3) Dependent's relationship to you	(4) ✓ If child under age 17 qualifying for child tax credit (see instructions)
			☐
			☐
			☐
			☐

If more than six dependents, see instructions.

Add numbers on lines above ▶ **1**

d Total number of exemptions claimed.

Income

Attach Form(s) W-2 here. Also attach Form(s) 1099-R if tax was withheld.

If you did not get a W-2, see instructions.

Enclose, but do not attach, any payment. Also, please use Form 1040-V.

7 Wages, salaries, tips, etc. Attach Form(s) W-2. ... 7 **28,000.**
8a Taxable interest. Attach Schedule B if required. ... 8a
 b Tax-exempt interest. **Do not** include on line 8a. 8b
9a Ordinary dividends. Attach Schedule B if required. ... 9a
 b Qualified dividends (see instructions). 9b
10 Capital gain distributions (see instructions). ... 10
11a IRA distributions. 11a 11b Taxable amount (see instructions). 11b
12a Pensions and annuities. 12a 12b Taxable amount (see instructions). 12b
13 Unemployment compensation and Alaska Permanent Fund dividends. 13
14a Social security benefits. 14a 14b Taxable amount (see instructions). 14b
15 Add lines 7 through 14b (far right column). This is your **total income.** ▶ 15 **28,000.**

Adjusted gross income
16 Educator expenses (see instructions). 16
17 IRA deduction (see instructions). 17
18 Student loan interest deduction (see instructions). 18
19 Tuition and fees. Attach Form 8917. 19
20 Add lines 16 through 19. These are your **total adjustments.** 20
21 Subtract line 20 from line 15. This is your **adjusted gross income.** ▶ 21 **28,000.**

For Disclosure, Privacy Act, and Paperwork Reduction Act Notice, see separate instructions. BAA
Form **1040A** (2011)
REV 12/01/11 TTW

Apprentice Tom
Pays Income Tax & Social Security / Medicare

Form 1040A (2011) — Page 2

Tax, credits, and payments	22	Enter the amount from line 21 (adjusted gross income).	22	28,000.
	23a	Check if: ☐ You were born before January 2, 1947, ☐ Blind ☐ Spouse was born before January 2, 1947, ☐ Blind } Total boxes checked ▶ 23a		
	b	If you are married filing separately and your spouse itemizes deductions, check here ▶ 23b ☐		
Standard Deduction for—	24	Enter your **standard deduction**.	24	5,800.
• People who check any box on line 23a or 23b **or** who can be claimed as a dependent, see instructions.	25	Subtract line 24 from line 22. If line 24 is more than line 22, enter -0-.	25	22,200.
	26	**Exemptions.** Multiply $3,700 by the number on line 6d.	26	3,700.
	27	Subtract line 26 from line 25. If line 26 is more than line 25, enter -0-. This is your **taxable income**. ▶	27	18,500.
• All others: Single or Married filing separately, $5,800	28	**Tax,** including any alternative minimum tax (see instructions).	28	2,354.
	29	Credit for child and dependent care expenses. Attach Form 2441.	29	
Married filing jointly or Qualifying widow(er), $11,600	30	Credit for the elderly or the disabled. Attach Schedule R.	30	
	31	Education credits from Form 8863, line 23.	31	
Head of household, $8,500	32	Retirement savings contributions credit. Attach Form 8880.	32	
	33	Child tax credit (see instructions).	33	
	34	Add lines 29 through 33. These are your **total credits.**	34	
	35	Subtract line 34 from line 28. If line 34 is more than line 28, enter -0-. This is your **total tax.**	35	2,354.
	36	Federal income tax withheld from Forms W-2 and 1099.	36	
If you have a qualifying child, attach Schedule EIC.	37	2011 estimated tax payments and amount applied from 2010 return.	37	
	38a	**Earned income credit (EIC).**	38a	
	b	Nontaxable combat pay election. 38b		
	39	Additional child tax credit. Attach Form 8812.	39	
	40	American opportunity credit from Form 8863, line 14.	40	
	41	Add lines 36, 37, 38a, 39, and 40. These are your **total payments.** ▶	41	
Refund	42	If line 41 is more than line 35, subtract line 35 from line 41. This is the amount you **overpaid.**	42	
Direct deposit? See instructions and fill in 43b, 43c, and 43d or Form 8888.	43a	Amount of line 42 you want **refunded to you.** If Form 8888 is attached, check here ▶ ☐	43a	
	▶ b	Routing number x x x x x x x x x ▶ c Type: ☐ Checking ☐ Savings		
	▶ d	Account number x x x x x x x x x x x x x x x x x		
	44	Amount of line 42 you want **applied to your 2012 estimated tax.**	44	
Amount you owe	45	**Amount you owe.** Subtract line 41 from line 35. For details on how to pay, see instructions. ▶	45	2,401.
	46	Estimated tax penalty (see instructions).	46	47.

Third party designee
Do you want to allow another person to discuss this return with the IRS (see instructions)? ☐ **Yes.** Complete the following. ☒ **No**
Designee's name ▶   Phone no. ▶   Personal identification number (PIN) ▶

Sign here
Joint return? See page 13. Keep a copy for your records.

Under penalties of perjury, I declare that I have examined this return and accompanying schedules and statements, and to the best of my knowledge and belief, they are true, correct, and accurately list all amounts and sources of income I received during the tax year. Declaration of preparer (other than the taxpayer) is based on all information of which the preparer has any knowledge.

Your signature	Date	Your occupation	Daytime phone number
		CARPENTER APPRENTICE	(888) 777-7777
Spouse's signature. If a joint return, **both** must sign.	Date	Spouse's occupation	If the IRS sent you an Identity Protection PIN, enter it here (see inst).

Paid preparer use only

Print/type preparer's name	Preparer's signature	Date	Check ☐ if self-employed	PTIN
Firm's name ▶ SELF PREPARED			Firm's EIN ▶	
Firm's address ▶			Phone no.	

REV 12/01/11 TTW   Form **1040A** (2011)

Appendix

Principal Business or Professional Activity Codes
IRS Job Classification Codes

These codes for the Principal Business or Professional Activity classify sole proprietorships by the type of activity they are engaged in to facilitate the administration of the Internal Revenue Code. These six-digit codes are based on the North American Industry Classification System (NAICS).

Select the category that best describes your primary business activity (for example, Real Estate). Then select the activity that best identifies the principal source of your sales or receipts (for example, real estate agent). Now find the six-digit code assigned to this activity (for example, 531210, the code for offices of real estate agents and brokers) and enter it on Schedule C or C-EZ, line B.

Note. If your principal source of income is from farming activities, you should file Schedule F.

Accommodation, Food Services, & Drinking Places

Accommodation
- 721310 Rooming & boarding houses
- 721210 RV (recreational vehicle) parks & recreational camps
- 721100 Traveler accommodation (including hotels, motels, & bed & breakfast inns)

Food Services & Drinking Places
- 722410 Drinking places (alcoholic beverages)
- 722110 Full-service restaurants
- 722210 Limited-service eating places
- 722300 Special food services (including food service contractors & caterers)

Administrative & Support and Waste Management & Remediation Services

Administrative & Support Services
- 561430 Business service centers (including private mail centers & copy shops)
- 561740 Carpet & upholstery cleaning services
- 561440 Collection agencies
- 561450 Credit bureaus
- 561410 Document preparation services
- 561300 Employment services
- 561710 Exterminating & pest control services
- 561210 Facilities support (management) services
- 561600 Investigation & security services
- 561920 Janitorial services
- 561730 Landscaping services
- 561110 Office administrative services
- 561420 Telephone call centers (including telephone answering services & telemarketing bureaus)
- 561500 Travel arrangement & reservation services
- 561490 Other business support services (including repossession services, court reporting, & stenotype services)
- 561790 Other services to buildings & dwellings
- 561900 Other support services (including packaging & labeling services, & convention & trade show organizers)

Waste Management & Remediation Services
- 562000 Waste management & remediation services

Agriculture, Forestry, Hunting, & Fishing
- 112900 Animal production (including breeding of cats and dogs)
- 114110 Fishing
- 113000 Forestry & logging (including forest nurseries & timber tracts)
- 114210 Hunting & trapping

Support Activities for Agriculture & Forestry
- 115210 Support activities for animal production (including farriers)
- 115110 Support activities for crop production (including cotton ginning, soil preparation, planting, & cultivating)
- 115310 Support activities for forestry

Arts, Entertainment, & Recreation

Amusement, Gambling, & Recreation Industries
- 713100 Amusement parks & arcades
- 713200 Gambling industries
- 713900 Other amusement & recreation services (including golf courses, skiing facilities, marinas, fitness centers, bowling centers, skating rinks, miniature golf courses)

Museums, Historical Sites, & Similar Institutions
- 712100 Museums, historical sites, & similar institutions

Performing Arts, Spectator Sports, & Related Industries
- 711410 Agents & managers for artists, athletes, entertainers, & other public figures
- 711510 Independent artists, writers, & performers
- 711100 Performing arts companies
- 711300 Promoters of performing arts, sports, & similar events
- 711210 Spectator sports (including professional sports clubs & racetrack operations)

Construction of Buildings
- 236200 Nonresidential building construction
- 236100 Residential building construction

Heavy and Civil Engineering Construction
- 237310 Highway, street, & bridge construction
- 237210 Land subdivision
- 237100 Utility system construction
- 237990 Other heavy & civil engineering construction

Specialty Trade Contractors
- 238310 Drywall & insulation contractors
- 238210 Electrical contractors
- 238350 Finish carpentry contractors
- 238330 Flooring contractors
- 238130 Framing carpentry contractors
- 238150 Glass & glazing contractors
- 238140 Masonry contractors
- 238320 Painting & wall covering contractors
- 238220 Plumbing, heating & air-conditioning contractors

Page # 1

Appendix
IRS Job Classification Codes

Principal Business or Professional Activity Codes (continued)

- 238110 Poured concrete foundation & structure contractors
- 238160 Roofing contractors
- 238170 Siding contractors
- 238910 Site preparation contractors
- 238120 Structural steel & precast concrete construction contractors
- 238340 Tile & terrazzo contractors
- 238290 Other building equipment contractors
- 238390 Other building finishing contractors
- 238190 Other foundation, structure, & building exterior contractors
- 238990 All other specialty trade contractors

Educational Services
- 611000 Educational services (including schools, colleges, & universities)

Finance & Insurance
Credit Intermediation & Related Activities
- 522100 Depository credit intermediation (including commercial banking, savings institutions, & credit unions)
- 522200 Nondepository credit intermediation (including sales financing & consumer lending)
- 522300 Activities related to credit intermediation (including loan brokers)

Insurance Agents, Brokers, & Related Activities
- 524210 Insurance agencies & brokerages
- 524290 Other insurance related activities

Securities, Commodity Contracts, & Other Financial Investments & Related Activities
- 523140 Commodity contracts brokers
- 523130 Commodity contracts dealers
- 523110 Investment bankers & securities dealers
- 523210 Securities & commodity exchanges
- 523120 Securities brokers
- 523900 Other financial investment activities (including investment advice)

Health Care & Social Assistance
Ambulatory Health Care Services
- 621610 Home health care services
- 621510 Medical & diagnostic laboratories
- 621310 Offices of chiropractors
- 621210 Offices of dentists
- 621330 Offices of mental health practitioners (except physicians)
- 621320 Offices of optometrists
- 621340 Offices of physical, occupational & speech therapists, & audiologists
- 621111 Offices of physicians (except mental health specialists)
- 621112 Offices of physicians, mental health specialists
- 621391 Offices of podiatrists
- 621399 Offices of all other miscellaneous health practitioners
- 621400 Outpatient care centers
- 621900 Other ambulatory health care services (including ambulance services, blood, & organ banks)

Hospitals
- 622000 Hospitals

Nursing & Residential Care Facilities
- 623000 Nursing & residential care facilities

Social Assistance
- 624410 Child day care services
- 624200 Community food & housing, & emergency & other relief services
- 624100 Individual & family services
- 624310 Vocational rehabilitation services

Information
- 511000 Publishing industries (except Internet)

Broadcasting (except Internet) & Telecommunications
- 515000 Broadcasting (except Internet)
- 517000 Telecommunications & Internet service providers

Data Processing Services
- 518210 Data processing, hosting, & related services
- 519100 Other information services (including news syndicates & libraries, Internet publishing & broadcasting)

Motion Picture & Sound Recording
- 512100 Motion picture & video industries (except video rental)
- 512200 Sound recording industries

Manufacturing
- 315000 Apparel mfg.
- 312000 Beverage & tobacco product mfg.
- 334000 Computer & electronic product mfg.
- 335000 Electrical equipment, appliance, & component mfg.
- 332000 Fabricated metal product mfg.
- 337000 Furniture & related product mfg.
- 333000 Machinery mfg.
- 339110 Medical equipment & supplies mfg.
- 322000 Paper mfg.
- 324100 Petroleum & coal products mfg.
- 326000 Plastics & rubber products mfg.
- 331000 Primary metal mfg.
- 323100 Printing & related support activities
- 313000 Textile mills
- 314000 Textile product mills
- 336000 Transportation equipment mfg.
- 321000 Wood product mfg.
- 339900 Other miscellaneous mfg.

Chemical Manufacturing
- 325100 Basic chemical mfg.
- 325500 Paint, coating, & adhesive mfg.
- 325300 Pesticide, fertilizer, & other agricultural chemical mfg.
- 325410 Pharmaceutical & medicine mfg.
- 325200 Resin, synthetic rubber, & artificial & synthetic fibers & filaments mfg.
- 325600 Soap, cleaning compound, & toilet preparation mfg.
- 325900 Other chemical product & preparation mfg.

Food Manufacturing
- 311110 Animal food mfg.
- 311800 Bakeries & tortilla mfg.
- 311500 Dairy product mfg.
- 311400 Fruit & vegetable preserving & speciality food mfg.
- 311200 Grain & oilseed milling
- 311610 Animal slaughtering & processing
- 311710 Seafood product preparation & packaging
- 311300 Sugar & confectionery product mfg.
- 311900 Other food mfg. (including coffee, tea, flavorings, & seasonings)

Leather & Allied Product Manufacturing
- 316210 Footwear mfg. (including leather, rubber, & plastics)
- 316110 Leather & hide tanning & finishing
- 316990 Other leather & allied product mfg.

Nonmetallic Mineral Product Manufacturing
- 327300 Cement & concrete product mfg.
- 327100 Clay product & refractory mfg.
- 327210 Glass & glass product mfg.
- 327400 Lime & gypsum product mfg.
- 327900 Other nonmetallic mineral product mfg.

Mining
- 212110 Coal mining
- 212200 Metal ore mining
- 212300 Nonmetallic mineral mining & quarrying
- 211110 Oil & gas extraction
- 213110 Support activities for mining

Other Services
Personal & Laundry Services
- 812111 Barber shops
- 812112 Beauty salons
- 812220 Cemeteries & crematories
- 812310 Coin-operated laundries & drycleaners
- 812320 Drycleaning & laundry services (except coin-operated) (including laundry & drycleaning dropoff & pickup sites)
- 812210 Funeral homes & funeral services
- 812330 Linen & uniform supply
- 812113 Nail salons
- 812930 Parking lots & garages
- 812910 Pet care (except veterinary) services
- 812920 Photofinishing
- 812190 Other personal care services (including diet & weight reducing centers)
- 812990 All other personal services

Repair & Maintenance
- 811120 Automotive body, paint, interior, & glass repair
- 811110 Automotive mechanical & electrical repair & maintenance
- 811190 Other automotive repair & maintenance (including oil change & lubrication shops & car washes)
- 811310 Commercial & industrial machinery & equipment (except automotive & electronic) repair & maintenance
- 811210 Electronic & precision equipment repair & maintenance
- 811430 Footwear & leather goods repair
- 811410 Home & garden equipment & appliance repair & maintenance
- 811420 Reupholstery & furniture repair
- 811490 Other personal & household goods repair & maintenance

Professional, Scientific, & Technical Services
- 541100 Legal services
- 541211 Offices of certified public accountants
- 541214 Payroll services
- 541213 Tax preparation services
- 541219 Other accounting services

Architectural, Engineering, & Related Services
- 541310 Architectural services
- 541350 Building inspection services
- 541340 Drafting services
- 541330 Engineering services
- 541360 Geophysical surveying & mapping services
- 541320 Landscape architecture services
- 541370 Surveying & mapping (except geophysical) services
- 541380 Testing laboratories

Computer Systems Design & Related Services
- 541510 Computer systems design & related services

Specialized Design Services
- 541400 Specialized design services (including interior, industrial, graphic, & fashion design)

Other Professional, Scientific, & Technical Services
- 541800 Advertising & related services
- 541600 Management, scientific, & technical consulting services
- 541910 Market research & public opinion polling
- 541920 Photographic services
- 541700 Scientific research & development services
- 541930 Translation & interpretation services
- 541940 Veterinary services
- 541990 All other professional, scientific, & technical services

Real Estate & Rental & Leasing
Real Estate
- 531100 Lessors of real estate (including miniwarehouses & self-storage units)
- 531210 Offices of real estate agents & brokers
- 531320 Offices of real estate appraisers
- 531310 Real estate property managers
- 531390 Other activities related to real estate

Rental & Leasing Services
- 532100 Automotive equipment rental & leasing
- 532400 Commercial & industrial machinery & equipment rental & leasing
- 532210 Consumer electronics & appliances rental
- 532220 Formal wear & costume rental

Appendix

Principal Business or Professional Activity Codes (continued) — IRS Job Classification Codes

532310 General rental centers
532230 Video tape & disc rental
532290 Other consumer goods rental

Religious, Grantmaking, Civic, Professional, & Similar Organizations
813000 Religious, grantmaking, civic, professional, & similar organizations

Retail Trade

Building Material & Garden Equipment & Supplies Dealers
444130 Hardware stores
444110 Home centers
444200 Lawn & garden equipment & supplies stores
444120 Paint & wallpaper stores
444190 Other building materials dealers

Clothing & Accessories Stores
448130 Children's & infants' clothing stores
448150 Clothing accessories stores
448140 Family clothing stores
448310 Jewelry stores
448320 Luggage & leather goods stores
448110 Men's clothing stores
448210 Shoe stores
448120 Women's clothing stores
448190 Other clothing stores

Electronic & Appliance Stores
443130 Camera & photographic supplies stores
443120 Computer & software stores
443111 Household appliance stores
443112 Radio, television, & other electronics stores

Food & Beverage Stores
445310 Beer, wine, & liquor stores
445220 Fish & seafood markets
445230 Fruit & vegetable markets
445100 Grocery stores (including supermarkets & convenience stores without gas)
445210 Meat markets
445290 Other specialty food stores

Furniture & Home Furnishing Stores
442110 Furniture stores
442200 Home furnishings stores

Gasoline Stations
447100 Gasoline stations (including convenience stores with gas)

General Merchandise Stores
452000 General merchandise stores

Health & Personal Care Stores
446120 Cosmetics, beauty supplies, & perfume stores
446130 Optical goods stores
446110 Pharmacies & drug stores
446190 Other health & personal care stores

Motor Vehicle & Parts Dealers
441300 Automotive parts, accessories, & tire stores
441222 Boat dealers
441221 Motorcycle dealers
441110 New car dealers
441210 Recreational vehicle dealers (including motor home & travel trailer dealers)
441120 Used car dealers
441229 All other motor vehicle dealers

Sporting Goods, Hobby, Book, & Music Stores
451211 Book stores
451120 Hobby, toy, & game stores
451140 Musical instrument & supplies stores
451212 News dealers & newsstands
451220 Prerecorded tape, compact disc, & record stores
451130 Sewing, needlework, & piece goods stores
451110 Sporting goods stores

Miscellaneous Store Retailers
453920 Art dealers
453110 Florists
453220 Gift, novelty, & souvenir stores
453930 Manufactured (mobile) home dealers
453210 Office supplies & stationery stores
453910 Pet & pet supplies stores
453310 Used merchandise stores
453990 All other miscellaneous store retailers (including tobacco, candle, & trophy shops)

Nonstore Retailers
454112 Electronic auctions
454111 Electronic shopping
454310 Fuel dealers
454113 Mail-order houses
454210 Vending machine operators
454390 Other direct selling establishments (including door-to-door retailing, frozen food-plan providers, party plan merchandisers, & coffee-break service providers)

Transportation & Warehousing
481000 Air transportation
485510 Charter bus industry
484110 General freight trucking, local
484120 General freight trucking, long distance
485210 Interurban & rural bus transportation
486000 Pipeline transportation
482110 Rail transportation
487000 Scenic & sightseeing transportation
485410 School & employee bus transportation
484200 Specialized freight trucking (including household moving vans)
485300 Taxi & limousine service
485110 Urban transit systems
483000 Water transportation
485990 Other transit & ground passenger transportation
488000 Support activities for transportation (including motor vehicle towing)

Couriers & Messengers
492000 Couriers & messengers

Warehousing & Storage Facilities
493100 Warehousing & storage (except lessors of miniwarehouses & self-storage units)

Utilities
221000 Utilities

Wholesale Trade

Merchant Wholesalers, Durable Goods
423600 Electrical & electronic goods
423200 Furniture & home furnishing
423700 Hardware & plumbing & heating equipment & supplies
423940 Jewelry, watch, precious stone, & precious metals
423300 Lumber & other construction materials
423800 Machinery, equipment, & supplies
423500 Metal & mineral (except petroleum)
423100 Motor vehicle & motor vehicle parts & supplies
423400 Professional & commercial equipment & supplies
423930 Recyclable materials
423910 Sporting & recreational goods & supplies
423920 Toy & hobby goods & supplies
423990 Other miscellaneous durable goods

Merchant Wholesalers, Nondurable Goods
424300 Apparel, piece goods, & notions
424800 Beer, wine, & distilled alcoholic beverage
424920 Books, periodicals, & newspapers
424600 Chemical & allied products
424210 Drugs & druggists' sundries
424500 Farm product raw materials
424910 Farm supplies
424930 Flower, nursery stock, & florists' supplies
424400 Grocery & related products
424950 Paint, varnish, & supplies
424100 Paper & paper products
424700 Petroleum & petroleum products
424940 Tobacco & tobacco products
424990 Other miscellaneous nondurable goods

Wholesale Electronic Markets and Agents & Brokers
425110 Business to business electronic markets
425120 Wholesale trade agents & brokers

999999 Unclassified establishments (unable to classify)

Suggested Resources for Further Information

1. *Waiting for Superman*—Video or book version—What parents can do.
2. *Liberating Learning*—Terry M. Moe and John E. Chubb—Advanced Academics Company.
3. *No They Can't—John Stossel.*
4. *NO APOLOGY: Believe in America, The Case for American Greatness.*
5. *www.apprentice101.com—Website.*

References

1. Clinton, Bill. 2011. *Back To Work: Why We Need Smart Government For A Strong Economy.* New York: Alfred A. Knopf.
2. Couch, Christina. 2012. *Is Education Worth The Debt?: Few Jobs For The Young.* www.finance.yahoo.com/news (4/23/12).
3. Guggenheim, Davis, Director. 2010. *Waiting For Superman: Film Documentary.* Sundance Film Festival.
4. Garofalo, Pat. 2012. *One Unemployed Youth Costs Taxpayers $14,000 Each Year.* www.thinkprogress.org/economy(1/18/12).
5. Honan, Edith. 2012. *College Students Protest Debt On "Trillion Dollar Day".* London: News@ reuters.com (4/26/12).
6. Newman, Rick. 2012. *How Student Debt Is Slowing The Recovery.* www.usnews.com/news(4/9/12).
7. North, Gary. 2012. *Subprime College Loans: $270 Billion.* www.garynorth.com/public (3/27/12).
8. Romney, Mitt. 2010. NO APOLOGY*: Believe in America.* The Case For American Greatness. New York: St. Martin's Griffen.
9. Stossel, John. 2012. *No, They Can't: Why Government Fails—But Individuals Succeed.* New York: Threshold Editions.
10. Tanner, Michael. 2012. *The Poverty Of Welfare: Helping Others In Civil Society.* Washington D.C.: Cato Institute.
11. Yen, Hope. (2012*). 1 IN 2 New Graduates Are Jobless Or Underemployed.* www.finance.yahoo.com/news(4/24/12).

12. Wikipedia. 2012. *Washington D.C. Opportunity Scholarship Program.* www.en.wikipedia.org/wiki/D.C._Opportunity_Scholarship_Program.
13. Wikipedia. 2012. *Great Society.* www.en.wikipedia.org/wiki/greatsociety.
14. Wikipedia. 2012. Apprenticeship. www.wikipedia.org/wiki/apprenticeship.
15. *National Center For Education Evaluation And Regional Assistance: Evaluation Of the D.C. Opportunity Scholarship Program: Executive Summary.* www.ies.ed.gov/ncee/pubs/20094050.
16. *The New Deal.* www.u-s-history.com (accessed 4/22/12).

About the Author

Arthur W. Hoffmann, Ed.D.;P.E. holds a Doctorate Degree from Western Michigan University in Educational Leadership and an MBA from Central Michigan University in Management & Supervision. Dr. Hoffmann is the owner and CEO of TEAM Resources, Inc. TEAM is an acronym for Technical, Engineering, Administrative & Management Resources, that contracts professional & technical personnel to the international automobile industry.

Dr. Hoffmann was instrumental in the development and training of "newly hired General Motors employees' orientation and training program", conducted in cooperation with Ferris State University, in Big Rapids, Michigan. More than 125 "new" employees successfully completed this technical "apprenticeship" program and are currently productive General Motors employees.

As an entrepreneur and CEO of TEAM, Dr. Hoffmann recruited and trained European and Asian Engineers to join the TEAM organization as part of a multi-national engineering group to service the U.S. and foreign automotive companies that have facilities in the United States. Currently Dr. Hoffmann is a consultant to the automotive industry. He has published several books, two of which are devoted to advancing automotive safety. They are: *"Don't be a Dummy"* and *"Precious Cargo"* both published by iUniverse, Inc., Bloomington, IN.

www.ingramcontent.com/pod-product-compliance
Lightning Source LLC
Chambersburg PA
CBHW030914180526
45163CB00004B/1835